ADOLESCENT
CATECHESIS

RESOURCES FROM THE LIVING LIGHT

UNITED STATES CONFERENCE OF CATHOLIC BISHOPS
Washington, D.C.

Articles in this resource collection *Adolescent Catechesis* were originally published in *The Living Light: An Interdisciplinary Review of Catholic Religious Education, Catechesis, and Pastoral Ministry*.

The Department of Education of the United States Conference of Catholic Bishops (USCCB) has sole responsibility for the editorial content of *The Living Light* in collaboration with members of the Department of Religion and Religious Education at The Catholic University of America. *The Living Light* is a professional journal, published with ecclesiastical approbation and authorized for publication by the undersigned.

Msgr. William P. Fay
General Secretary, USCCB

Table of Contents

Dear Reader,

Welcome to the first issue of a new series, *Resources from "The Living Light."* This pastoral resource from the United States Conference of Catholic Bishops (USCCB) is designed as a collection of key articles—some written over a number of years—on a given topic in Catholic religious education, catechesis, and youth and pastoral ministry. All texts have been published in past editions of the interdisciplinary journal *The Living Light.*

A strength of *The Living Light* is the excellent scholarly coverage of topics of interest to those whose ministries touch upon catechesis. We hope that Catholic parish and school catechists, directors and coordinators of religious education and youth ministry, members of parish faith formation teams, pastoral associates, liturgists, and young adult ministers will look to *The Living Light* and *Resources from "The Living Light"* as primary sources of information for pastoral praxis.

Forthcoming issues of this series will focus on topics such as evangelization, adult faith formation, sacramental preparation, and theology.

We would like to hear from readers about how we can make this series helpful to your ministry, whether it be in a parish or educational/academic setting.

In the meantime, may God bless you in your work or studies, and may you be enlightened by your reading.

USCCB Publishing

Adolescent Catechesis

WHOSE RESPONSIBILITY?

By BERARD L. MARTHALER

Executive Editor, *The Living Light*

One thing is clear in the field of youth ministry: responsibility for adolescent catechesis at the national, diocesan, and parish levels has become muddled. When parish DREs are asked, "Do you do adolescent catechesis in your program?" most answer, "No, that's the responsibility of the youth minister." When youth ministers are asked the same question, they are likely to respond that it is the responsibility of the DRE.

WHY THE CONFUSION?

One answer is to see the confusion as an administrative problem—everybody's responsibility is no one's responsibility. A few years ago, the USCC (now USCCB) moved youth ministry from the Department of Education to what is now the Secretariat for Family, Laity, Women, and Youth. The administrative change, designed to better serve the model of comprehensive youth ministry then

coming into vogue, had a ripple effect that reached diocesan offices. The unforeseen result, felt most acutely at the parish level, was a distancing of youth ministry from the religious education (catechetical) office, making it a freestanding endeavor. The job description for youth ministers, more often than not, did not require the applicant to have any formal training in religious education/catechetics. Nor did the job description of DREs indicate that they would have oversight of or be expected to contribute to the youth ministry program.

Another reason for the confusion is the lack of a clear understanding of the goals of adolescent catechesis and youth ministry. How do they relate to one another? Is it the responsibility of youth ministers themselves to catechize? Or is it enough for them to create a context and present opportunities (recreational outings, retreats, etc.) where catechesis might occur? Should adolescent catechesis be formal and systematic or occasional and timely?

Some years ago when the formal structures of the Confraternity of Christian Doctrine (CCD) were still in place, a friend came to me for help. Her assistant pastor who doubled as youth minister had asked her to design a series of courses for the CCD program held on Wednesday nights. The participants were students (ninth through twelfth grades) in the neighboring high schools. Each session consisted of two forty-minute classes with a forty-minute break in between. My friend was to develop the contents—the scope and sequence—for the two class periods. I asked her why she did not consult with the assistant pastor. Her response: "Oh, he doesn't care what we teach. His interest is in the interval between classes when the young people socialize and get to know one another as members of the parish. Oh, yes, and it is an opportunity for Catholic boys to meet Catholic girls." Who was doing adolescent catechesis? My friend who decided on what to teach? The CCD teacher in the classroom? The assistant pastor with his informal (but planned) interaction with the kids during intermission?

Fifteen years ago when *A Vision of Youth Ministry* was written, the authors assumed adolescence to be a stage of life one passes through on the way to adulthood, though they were not clear about whether it is chiefly a matter of emotional, psychological, or social development. In any case, in the era of the CCD, it was generally accepted that most individuals had grown out of it by the time they reached seventeen or eighteen. In the last few years, "adolescence" is being redefined. The Society for Adolescent Medicine, a physicians' organization, states that its members care for persons "10 to 26" years of age. The MacArthur Foundation is funding a multi-million dollar project called Transitions to Adulthood. It pegs the terminus of that transition at thirty-four years of age. Frank F. Furstenberg Jr., a professor at the University of Pennsylvania, noted in the January 2, 2002, issue of the *Washington Post* that it is to the advantage of commercial interests—merchandisers of clothing, recording artists, and the media in general—to expand their market by convincing young people (and their elders) that adolescence does not end with teens.

The *Washington Post* quotes Furstenberg: "Adolescence has been stretched so much it's becoming an obsolescent term." If this indeed is the case, how is adolescent catechesis to be understood? What are its goals? Do we have the right question when we ask how it relates to youth ministry? Might it be that the question should be how youth ministry relates to the community? Is it feasible that a catechumenal model might be developed that would foster a symbiotic relationship between adolescent catechesis and youth ministry, and between them and the parish community as a whole? In this model, adolescent catechesis becomes everyone's responsibility, but the need remains for someone—a specific person or office—to design the program and see that it is made to work. ❧

Evangelizing Catechesis and Comprehensive Youth Ministry

Recent church documents situate youth ministry in two different frameworks. Both are compelling and, in the end, complementary.

By MAURA THOMPSON HAGARTY AND MICHAEL J. HAGARTY

C atechesis, especially the catechesis of youth, can tax the parish minister. Parish ministry today can be fragmented and compartmentalized when the collaboration among leaders is limited to calendar meetings and does not extend to working together to establish a common, unifying vision. Typical parish structures can tend to separate the Church's ministries and segregate people according to age. In order to be effective, both youth ministry and catechesis depend on communication between leaders, connections between ministries, and relationships among all the generations. The Church has invested significant energy in clarifying and communicating visions for pastoral ministry in official directories and statements, including two recent documents that address adolescent catechesis: *Renewing the Vision: A Framework for Catholic Youth Ministry* (RTV) and the *General Directory for Catechesis* (GDC).[1] Because of their differences, these documents could impede the very communication and collaboration that are required to make youth catechesis effective and meaningful. This does not, however, need to happen. What would happen in parishes if the youth ministry leaders—grounded in the vision of comprehensive youth ministry articulated in RTV—and the catechetical leaders—rooted in the GDC's vision of evangelizing catechesis—sat down together to listen, to learn, and to work toward greater collaboration in their efforts to build the reign of God? What would they discuss?

The visions of both "evangelizing catechesis" and "comprehensive youth ministry" operative in the Church's ministry today situate youth catechesis within compelling, but different, integrative frameworks. The GDC highlights six tasks of catechesis and contextualizes the whole of catechesis within the process of evangelization. RTV presents a framework for integration comprising three goals, eight components, and a number of themes within which catechesis is situated. This essay aims to help pastoral leaders explore the nature and relationship of these visions and their roles in guiding the Church's catechetical efforts with youth. Are they complementary, each making a contribution leading to a whole? Does it make a practical difference if pastoral leaders approach youth catechesis primarily from the perspective of the GDC rather than RTV or vice versa?

U.S. CATHOLIC CHURCH STATEMENTS ON YOUTH MINISTRY

A little more than twenty-five years ago the Department of Education of the United States Catholic Conference, in its statement *A Vision of Youth Ministry* (VYM), affirmed what many involved in ministry with youth were discovering: the most effective youth ministry is a multifaceted effort that integrates a number of key components.[2] This vision is rooted in the conviction that single-focus approaches—such as those used in sports, community building, or religious education—are less effective and should not be emphasized as much as comprehensive approaches comprising a variety of activities and strategies.[3] A central conviction fueling this shift concerned youth catechesis. Many adult leaders found that their catechetical efforts were more successful if they were viewed and carried out within a broad youth ministry framework. In 1975 Michael Warren remarked that "one might argue persuasively that the move to integrate youth catechesis into the broader pastoral field of youth ministry is the most significant development for youth catechesis since the rapid growth of youth retreats in the mid-1960s."[4] A number of dioceses ended the practice of dividing youth ministry offerings between separate CYO (Catholic Youth Organization) and CCD (Confraternity of Christian Doctrine) offices by establishing offices of youth ministry. Others sought to strengthen relationships among the various staff members and offices whose work touched youth. Many parishes also shifted to a more comprehensive approach to ministry with youth by taking age-group slices out of each of its ministries (i.e., religious education, social justice, prayer and worship, community life) and bringing them together under one leader or leadership team with a primary focus on youth. In many cases, the responsibility for youth catechesis shifted from DREs to youth ministers.

The move toward situating catechesis within the context of youth ministry meant more than changing organizational structures and leadership roles. This emerging vision put emphasis on the relationships between youth and adults.

Warren further noted that "what the young need today are not adults who will hand over information, but adults who will in a sense hand over themselves and the secret of their own faith. . . . Adolescents need adults who are willing to take the time to enter their lives and walk along with them in a journey of faith" (15). There was a growing awareness that youth benefit when adults treat them in a holistic way and recognize that their needs are interrelated. The 1976 statement of vision presented the Emmaus story (Lk 24:13-35) as a model of the dynamic at the heart of youth ministry. Jesus' way of relating to the disciples suggested the kind of presence and relationship that enable youth to grow in faith.

Five years ago the Catholic bishops of the United States issued *Renewing the Vision*, which builds on VYM by revising the framework it proposed. The renewed vision emphasizes that the entire community is responsible for youth ministry and calls youth to discipleship, active participation in the Church's mission, and healthy personal and spiritual development. RTV continues to situate catechesis within the broad framework of youth ministry and identifies it as one of the major components of it.[5]

The U.S. Catholic bishops' sense that youth catechesis needs renewal, expressed in RTV, is echoed by others. The GDC, concerned about pre-adolescents who celebrate confirmation and then almost immediately abandon the practice of Christian faith, asserts that "youth catechesis must be profoundly revised and revitalized" (no. 181). A recent newsletter of the National Conference for Catechetical Leadership (NCCL) reports on data from the *2001 Official Catholic Directory* (a.k.a. the *Kenedy Directory*) indicating that the number of youth enrolled in high school religious education programs continues to decline.[6]

A recent CARA (Center for Applied Research in the Apostolate) research study, which sought to identify model youth ministry programs in the United States, indicates that parish and diocesan leaders' views of the state of youth catechesis vary widely.[7] Leaders were asked to comment on how each of the components of youth ministry, as delineated in RTV, is carried out in their local setting. The responses regarding catechesis were far-ranging. At one end of the spectrum, leaders reported that catechesis was a weak aspect of youth ministry. For example, comments by diocesan leaders about catechesis included the following:

Nearly every parish does catechesis, but it is often removed from youth ministry. (65)
Some parishes, not the majority, offer catechesis to youth. (49)
This is the least engaged item in terms of a systematic endeavor with adolescents. (54)
One of the weaker areas . . . programming needs deepening. (70)

Others reported strong catechesis, citing regular programs and retreats, and explained that they try to catechize in every event. For example, a parish leader commented that "catechesis touches nearly everything they do, and is integrated into all their activities" (80). A diocesan leader, referring to a retreat program, remarked that "they try to do catechesis in a way that youth do not even realize they are doing it" (59). CARA found that, in programs judged to be models of effective youth ministry,

> many youth ministers are very aware of the interconnectedness of the eight components of *Renewing the Vision*. They strive to create programs which are organically comprehensive, in which one component reinforces and flows into the others. They understand that each event in a program can contain all eight components, even if the theme of the event focuses on just one. In particular, they often speak about how community, catechesis, prayer, and evangelization are part of everything they do in their youth ministry program. (3)

For its 1996 study *New Directions in Youth Ministry*, CARA surveyed more than six thousand participants in parish-based youth ministry programs. The youth reported that "they take part in a variety of parish activities . . . most especially religious education (59 percent), youth retreats (38 percent) and social events (37 percent)"(Froehle, 3). In response to questions about what they felt was emphasized in their parish youth ministry, they ranked religious education and the providing of a safe and caring place the highest.

THE FRAMEWORKS OF EVANGELIZING CATECHESIS AND COMPREHENSIVE YOUTH MINISTRY

The GDC and RTV stand in a long line of official church documents intended to guide the practices of pastoral leaders. Both the visions of evangelizing catechesis and comprehensive youth ministry put particular emphasis on the role of the community in fostering faith, stress evangelization and mission, and call for the integration of catechesis with numerous essential elements of Christian life. Both also call for the renewal of youth catechesis and offer guidance toward that end. After briefly summarizing central aspects of evangelizing catechesis and comprehensive youth ministry, as set forth in the GDC and RTV, we will discuss some implications for envisioning youth catechesis.

General Directory for Catechesis

The definitive aim of catechesis is the same as that of all evangelizing activity—communion with Jesus. Catechesis, a moment within the whole process of evangelization, "matures initial conversion to make it into a living, explicit and fruitful confession of faith" and helps people "renew the commitments [that conversion] entails" (no. 82). Catechesis accomplishes these objectives through diverse interrelated tasks that correspond to different dimensions of Christian life and faith. The GDC delineates six tasks: (1) to deepen knowledge of the faith by introducing the disciples of Jesus to a knowledge of Tradition and

Scripture; (2) to provide a liturgical education that brings the faithful to full, conscious, and active participation in liturgy; (3) to provide a moral formation that transmits Jesus' attitudes to the faithful in a way that leads to interior transformation; (4) to teach people to pray in such a way that catechesis is permeated by a climate of prayer; (5) to prepare the Christian to live in community; and (6) to prepare Christians to participate actively in the life and mission of the Church (nos. 85-86). "All of these tasks are necessary. . . . When catechesis omits one of these elements, the Christian faith does not attain full development. . . . These tasks are interdependent and develop together" (no. 87). The GDC cites canon 773 in identifying two principle means by which catechesis accomplishes these tasks: transmission of the gospel message and experience of the Christian life (no. 87). Liturgical education, for example, must explain what "liturgy" and "sacraments" are and also must "offer an experience of the different kinds of celebration and it must make symbols, gestures, etc. known and loved" (no. 87). The inclusion of experience of Christian life as a means of catechesis emphasizes the critically important role of the community members, who through their witness of a Christian way of life enable young people to enter into apprentice-type relationships essential for growth in faith.

Specifically regarding catechesis for young people, the GDC indicates some general directives that include remembering the diversity in religious situations of young people and recognizing that the most successful catechesis is that which is contextualized in the wider pastoral care of young people, especially when it addresses the problems affecting their lives (no. 184). The GDC emphasizes that the religious situation of young people often calls for reaching out to them with love, witnessing to a Christian way of life, and providing a first proclamation of the Gospel in order to prepare them for the strictly catechetical moment within the whole process of evangelization.

Renewing the Vision

Catechesis is identified as one of eight components of youth ministry, which together form the basis of an integrated approach aimed at accomplishing three goals:

Goal 1: To empower young people to live as disciples of Jesus Christ in our world today.

Goal 2: To draw young people to responsible participation in the life, mission, and work of the Catholic faith community.

Goal 3: To foster the total personal and spiritual growth of each young person. (9-18)

Catechesis helps young people "develop a deeper relationship with Jesus Christ and the Christian community, and increase their knowledge of the core content of the Catholic faith" (29). It helps them "enrich and expand their understanding of the Scriptures and the sacred tradition and their application to life today, and live more faithfully as disciples . . . especially through a life of prayer, justice, and loving service" (29). Catechesis is concerned with the whole person and with the fostering of faith in all three dimensions—trusting (heart), knowing and believing (mind), and doing (will). RTV calls for the involvement of all Catholic youth in some program of catechesis and identifies characteristics of effective catechetical programming for youth:

- Provides developmentally appropriate content and processes
- Teaches the core content of the Catholic faith as presented in the *Catechism of the Catholic Church*
- Integrates knowledge with the development of skills for living the faith
- Fosters dialogue between the life experiences of adolescents and the wisdom of Catholic faith
- Engages adolescents in the learning process through a variety of learning methods and activities and incorporates a variety of program approaches
- Fosters an environment conducive to hearing God's call, searching, questioning, expressing one's own point of view, and responding in faith to the call
- Provides for real-life applications of learning
- Promotes family faith development
- Recognizes and celebrates multicultural diversity
- Invites adolescents to explore the possibility of a personal call to ministry (29-30)

RTV suggests that catechesis is most effective when the developmental needs and life experiences of young people are used as the basis for selecting themes or topics for learning programs. It makes recommendations, organized according to the structure of the *Catechism of the Catholic Church*, for both younger and older adolescents.

DISCERNING THE DIRECTION FOR THE FUTURE

Both *Renewing the Vision* and the *General Directory for Catechesis* provide invaluable guidance for the Church's ministry with youth, including the renewal of catechesis. The full benefit of these documents, however, depends on dialogue between pastoral leaders. Below we highlight several themes that may help leaders interpret, integrate, and implement the visions of the two documents. Following each theme are questions that may be useful to parish leaders working to bring about effective youth catechesis.

Defining Terms

Two people conversing about the renewal of catechesis may misunderstand each other if one is immersed in RTV and the other in the GDC. It is essential that the Church's ministry with youth is supported in a wide array of ministry areas by pastoral leaders who are able to communicate and collaborate with one another. Paying attention to the meanings of key terms is crucial. Both documents suggest that catechesis is a complex endeavor and stress the interrelation of catechesis with other aspects of ministry. There are, however, important differences between the documents' uses of two key terms: "evangelization" and "catechesis." The youth ministry document RTV identifies *evangelization* as one of the eight components and describes it as the proclamation of the Gospel through the community's pronouncement and living witness. It involves witness, outreach, proclamation, invitation, conversion, and discipleship. RTV presents catechesis as a component distinct from evangelization and talks about it primarily in terms of learning programs. The GDC, in contrast, defines evangelization more broadly as a process that parallels the individual's journey from initial hearing of the Gospel and conversion to maturity of faith and active commitment to the Church's mission in the world. *Catechesis*, in the GDC, is one moment in the whole process of evangelization, which the GDC describes in terms of the following six stages:

- Transforms the temporal order, appropriating and renewing all cultures through charity
- Witnesses the Christian way of being and living
- Explicitly proclaims the Gospel
- Initiates into the faith and the Christian life through catechesis and the sacraments of initiation
- Nourishes communion among the faithful by means of continuous education in the faith (homilies and other forms of catechesis), the sacraments, and the practice of charity
- Arouses mission, sending all the disciples to proclaim the Gospel by word and deed (no. 48)

Defining catechesis in relation to the multi-stage process means that catechesis is preceded by certain pastoral activities, is accompanied by others, and ideally leads to mission. It also means that catechesis, like evangelization, is a ministry of word and witness, making use of the dual means of formation in doctrine and experience of Christian living. The GDC gives special emphasis to this second means of formation when it states that catechists do not yet have a full understanding of the concept of catechesis as "an initiation and apprenticeship in the entire Christian life" (no. 30). While the witness and apprenticeship implied by the phrase "experience of Christian living" are critically important to youth ministry, in contrast, RTV does not emphasize this experience in the same manner. Instead of addressing the witness of Christian life as a constitutive part of catechesis, as does the GDC, RTV addresses it in the descriptions of components distinct from catechesis, especially the ministries of community, evangelization, leadership development, and advocacy. For example, in its explanation of the ministry of community, RTV states that "to teach compassion, generosity, tolerance, peace, forgiveness, acceptance, and love as gospel values and to identify ourselves as Christians require us to live these values in our interactions with young people and in our community life" (34). It also highlights, in its description of evangelization, the importance of "offering ourselves and our community of faith as living models of the Christian faith in practice" (37).[8]

The differences between the two documents in this regard rest in different understandings of what constitutes catechesis and what is part of the context of catechesis. In light of the importance both place on the vitality of the context of catechesis, this is not necessarily a significant difference. In fact, clear lines of distinction between catechesis and other aspects of ministry are possible only in theory. Without attention to the meaning of terms, however, pastoral leaders may end up in conflicts over catechesis that mask both fundamental agreements and the true nature of genuine differences.

SUGGESTED QUESTIONS FOR REFLECTION
- How are the terms "evangelization" and "catechesis" used in your parish?
- What other terms are used in your local setting to describe these ministries?
- What activities or strategies are carried out in the practice of these ministries?
- Is evangelization, as presented in the GDC, another way of naming "comprehensive ministry with youth"?
- What implications do the visions of the GDC and RTV have for youth catechesis in your parish?

The Context of Catechesis

Both the GDC and RTV clearly demonstrate that the renewal of catechesis is intrinsically related to the renewal of the Church and all of its ministries. The two contextualize catechesis in distinct but complementary frameworks that relate catechesis to numerous essential dimensions of Christian life and the Church's mission. The frameworks remind pastoral leaders that the evaluation and planning necessary for effective catechesis go beyond catechesis to include consideration of the multifaceted context in which it is carried out. The visions of the two documents challenge any tendency to prematurely conclude that problems with the commitment of youth to the Church indicate problems primarily with youth catechesis—instead isolating catechesis as either the source of the concern or the arena in which it should be addressed.

SUGGESTED QUESTIONS FOR REFLECTION
- Have the youth experienced the Church as a community marked by charity and love?
- Do youth have the opportunity for relationships with family and commnity members who witness a Christian way of life?
- Have they heard the Gospel proclaimed in a manner adapted to their sociocultural and religious situations and experienced initial conversion?

THE FOLLOWING ADDITIONAL SET OF QUESTIONS, DRAWN FROM BOTH THE GDC AND RTV, IS A SAMPLING OF CONTEXT-RELATED ISSUES TO CONSIDER IN EVALUATING AND PLANNING FOR YOUTH CATECHESIS:
- Is the Church utilizing all of its ministries in its work with youth?
- What is going on in families with youth? Are we working to enhance ou partnerships with parents in developing the faith life of their adolescent children?
- To what extent is the whole community taking responsibility for ministry with youth?
- Do youth have opportunities for meaningful involvement in parish life and for the development of intergenerational relationships?
- To what extent is adult catechesis the axis around which youth catechesis revolves?

The Tasks of Catechesis

One of the most significant aspects of the six-task framework delineated in the GDC is the implication that integration is essential to catechesis. While catechesis is closely coordinated with all the other elements of the Church's ministry with youth, the six tasks emphasize that catechesis itself serves to develop and maintain the interrelation of all the dimensions of Christian life. RTV also conveys this sense of a web of relationships: "Each ministry component supports and enhances the others" (26). What the task framework can contribute to the vision of youth ministry is a way to talk in greater depth about how catechesis supports and enhances the other aspects of Christian life and ministry.

One caution to pastoral leaders is to avoid reducing the six tasks to themes or topics to be addressed in learning programs. Frameworks for pastoral ministry that are easy to remember and repeat (e.g., four pillars, six tasks, eight components) can become separated from the principles necessary for their correct interpretation and then can cease to function as effective summaries of the broader and more complete, if less verbally concise, understandings of the many elements that must be held together. If the six tasks do not remain rooted in the GDC's overall approach to catechesis, attempts to incorporate them effectively into the vision of comprehensive youth ministry will fail. The GDC's derivation of four of the six tasks from the now familiar four-pillar structure that was used to organize the presentation of doctrine in the *Catechism of the Catholic Church* may inadvertently contribute to this tendency to view the tasks as topics. Pastoral leaders who tend to think of doctrinal summaries when they see references to the *Catechism*'s structure are reminded that the GDC uses the pillars to organize the tasks because they correspond to dimensions of Christian life and that their role in organizing doctrine is rooted in the conviction that "there is an organic connection between our spiritual life and the dogmas" (*Catechism of the Catholic Church*, no. 89).

A second caution in implementing the six tasks is not to overlook the significance of the dual means identified by the GDC. The full implications of the directory's tasks will be missed if not rooted in the idea that catechesis utilizes the transmission of the gospel message as well as the experience of the Christian life to accomplish its tasks. The tasks of catechesis relate to word and witness, classroom and community, and doctrinal summaries and truths embodied in people's lives, as well as knowing and doing. The consideration of how the GDC's tasks of catechesis relate to comprehensive youth ministry must not overlook the fact that some aspects of catechesis as understood in the GDC, especially those related to the second means, are presented in RTV as parts of a number of components other than catechesis.

SUGGESTED QUESTIONS FOR REFLECTION

- How does the GDC's identification of six tasks of catechesis relate to your understanding of catechesis and the practices of catechesis in your parish?
- Does the emphasis on witness and adult relationships in the GDC and RTV have implications for the way youth catechesis is carried out in your parish?
- What's going on with adult faith formation in your parish, and what are the implications for youth catechesis?

An Alternative Framework of Tasks of Youth Catechesis

As RTV explains, a variety of schemata identify the ministries of the Church, and a variety of names describe each ministry. The GDC's six tasks and RTV's eight components are similar in that both schemata are drawn from frameworks that summarize the multifaceted life and mission of the Christian community.

It may be straightforward and logical to conclude that the integration of the GDC and RTV is best accomplished by incorporating the six tasks of catechesis into the RTV's discussion of catechesis. An alternative for pastoral leaders to consider is whether an effective integration of the insights of the two documents might be achieved by relating the key concept behind the six-task framework to the schema used in the youth ministry document. In other words, according to the GDC, catechesis fosters the maturation of Christian life by cultivating it in all its dimensions. In light of this, the GDC derives a task for catechesis from each of six dimensions. The particular way the directory describes and categorizes the dimensions of Christian life is secondary. Perhaps applying the central insight embodied in the task framework to the eight-component schema that has come to define comprehensive youth ministry in the United States would yield an effective alternative to envision the tasks of youth catechesis. A task for catechesis would be derived from each of the components. For example, the ministry of advocacy suggests the following task for youth catechesis: to prepare youth for this ministry by empowering them with the knowledge, skills, and attitudes necessary to shape society through speaking out and taking responsibility for the public issues that affect the lives of young people, children, and all those needing protection and support. Perhaps this alternate way of formulating and talking about tasks of youth catechesis would prove useful especially for parishes committed to fully implementing the vision of comprehensive youth ministry.

Both the GDC and RTV are rooted in the conviction that ministry efforts are intended to further Jesus' mission by empowering more and more people and communities to carry it out in the world. The critical question for pastoral leaders is whether the Church's ministries—regardless of how they are named, categorized, or coordinated—achieve this end.

Analysis of the Situation

Both the GDC and RTV call for paying attention to young people and the many dimensions—social, economic, cultural, religious—of their lives. The GDC uses the parable of the sower and the metaphor of soil, and challenges people working with youth to draw from the numerous fields that shed light on the lives of youth today. The analysis includes listening to the culture of youth in particular settings to discern "an echo (omen, invocation, sign) of the word of God; a discernment of what has an authentic Gospel value or is at least open to the Gospel" (no. 204). This must go beyond the conclusions of published research to incorporate the insights of the laity, pastoral workers, and clergy who live in the same cultural circumstance. The GDC expresses particular concern for language and young people:

One of the difficulties to be addressed and resolved is the question of "language" (mentality, sensibility, tastes, style, vocabulary) between young people and the Church (catechesis, catechists). A necessary "adaptation of catechesis to young people" is urged, in order to translate into their terms "the message of Jesus with patience and wisdom and without betrayal." (no. 185)

Renewing the Vision underlines the importance of carrying out ministry with adolescents in ways that are responsive to the diverse needs and circumstances of youth today. RTV notes a number of changes in our society that present new challenges, including the neglect of young people in America, consumerism, and the effects of the entertainment media. Too many families lack sufficient time together; too many communities lack the infrastructure necessary for promoting strong families and positive adolescent development. The bishops draw on social science research in their assessment that youth ministry has had a positive impact on the lives of young people and also in their portrayal of healthy adolescent development based on four essential building blocks or assets—knowledge, values, skills, and commitments—that make a significant difference in the lives of youth.

The broad diversity of the situations of youth today highlights the need for equally diverse approaches to ministry with adolescents. RTV stresses the need for parishes to develop flexible and adaptable program structures responsive to the varied situations and changing needs of youth and their families within their particular communities (25). The GDC discusses many forms of catechesis and calls for the development of new ways to carry out youth catechesis (no. 185).

The general directory and the U.S. bishops' youth ministry document both offer a vision rather than a blueprint for youth catechesis. There are no shortcuts to vibrant, effective ministry with adolescents. Catechesis is to be carried out in a wide variety of ways that correspond to the particular situations of youth in local settings. This implies the need for serious commitment to preliminary work, for collaboration and communication among leaders, and for significant relationships between youth and adults. While not easy, the effort this entails promises to lead more young people to a life of discipleship and active participation in the Church's mission in the world. &

1. National Conference of Catholic Bishops, *Renewing the Vision: A Framework for Catholic Youth Ministry* (Washington, D.C.: United States Catholic Conference, 1997); Congregation for the Clergy, *General Directory for Catechesis* (Washington, D.C.: United States Catholic Conference, 1997). Subsequent references are given in the text.

2. Department of Education, United States Catholic Conference, *A Vision of Youth Ministry* (Washington, D.C.: United States Catholic Conference, 1976). The 1976 statement identified seven components: word (including evangelization and catechesis), worship, the creation of community, guidance and healing, justice and service, enablement, and advocacy.

3. A recent study affirms the value of this conviction for the Church's ministry with adolescents. See Bryan Froehle, *New Directions in Youth Ministry: A National Study of Catholic Youth Ministry Program Participants* (Washington, D.C.: Center for Applied Research in the Apostolate [CARA] and the National Federation for Catholic Youth Ministry [NFCYM], 1996), 6. Subsequent references are given in the text.

4. Michael Warren, *A Future for Youth Catechesis* (New York: Paulist, 1975), 12. Subsequent references are given in the text.

5. RTV identifies eight components of youth ministry: advocacy, catechesis, community, evangelization, justice and service, leadership development, pastoral care, and prayer and worship.

6. See the Fall 2001 issue of the NCCL newsletter *Catechetical Leadership*.

7. Mary E. Bendyna, Mary L. Gautier, and Dominic J. Perri, *Model Youth Ministry Programs: A Report Prepared for the Saint Meinrad School of Theology* (Washington, D.C.: CARA, 2001). Subsequent references are given in the text.

8. The critical role of witness and apprenticeship for youth ministry is also developed in NFCYM's *The Challenge of Catholic Youth Evangelization: Called to be Witnesses and Storytellers* (Washington, D.C.: NFCYM, 1993).

The Spiritual Significance of the Nicodemus Narrative to Youth Ministry

The appeal that the Nicodemus Narrative has for adolescents is found in the emphasis it puts on starting fresh, encountering God, and growing in the Spirit.

By ARTHUR D. CANALES

atholic adolescents have often been troubled by the question asked by their evangelical friends at school: "Are you a born again Christian?" Puzzled, they ask themselves or respond, "I am Catholic. Can I be 'born again'?" The phrase "born again" is not a popular expression within Catholic circles; in fact, it can be easily misconstrued. Nevertheless, the phrase is extremely rich with deep spiritual significance that can foster spiritual renewal in adolescents. This phrase finds its source in a specific translation of a pericope of John's gospel:

> In reply Jesus declared, "I tell you the truth, no one can see the kingdom of God unless he is *born again*." "How can a man be born when he is old?" Nicodemus asked. "Surely he cannot enter a second time into his mother's womb to be born!" Jesus answered, "I tell you the truth, no one can enter the kingdom of God unless he is born of water and the Spirit. Flesh gives birth to flesh, but the Spirit gives birth to spirit. You should not be surprised at my saying, 'You must be *born again*.' The wind blows wherever it pleases. You hear its sound, but you cannot tell where it comes from or where it is going. So it is with everyone born of the Spirit." (Jn 3:3-8; italics added)[1]

This article will examine the role the Nicodemus Narrative above can play in the catechesis of adolescents. After the pastoral significance and catechetical relevance of the narrative are demonstrated, some practical examples of employing this narrative in your work will be presented. The hope is to remove the fear that often accompanies "born again" language and reintroduce the idea to Catholics as they prepare to receive the fire of the Holy Spirit.

Although the terminology "born again" is more closely associated with Evangelical, Pentecostal, and Charismatic churches, it is important to all Christians. Jesus does not tell Nicodemus simply to become "born again." Jesus confronts Nicodemus with an injunction to *be* "born again." The theological reality of being "born again" or having new life in Christ or rebirth is *regeneration*. Theologically, for Catholics, being "born again" happens during the sacrament of baptism. Catholics experience the spiritual edification and exhortation of being "born again" in the waters of baptism. As the Apostle Paul states, "We were therefore buried with [Christ] through baptism into death in order that, just as Christ was raised from the dead through the glory of the Father, we too may live a new life [in Christ]" (Rom 6:4). To profess being a Catholic is to declare one's celebration of the sacraments of initiation; therefore, it is a confession of being "born again."

The Catholic experience of becoming "born again" takes place during baptism. The self-expression and self-articulation of being "born again" is actually a post-baptismal phenomenon. It is a religious event, a religious experience—for most, a peak religious experience. Jesus was communicating the need to become "born again" to Nicodemus, a pious Jewish man living in first-century Palestine. Neither Jesus nor Nicodemus had any inkling of the religion known as Christianity. Jesus' use of the term "born again" can be interpreted as a religious encounter between God and the non-believer and/or non-Christian. To speak of a baptized person's being "born again" is un-scriptural! In order for the "born again" experience to be truly valid today, it must take place in the life of an unbaptized person.

THE PASTORAL RELEVANCE FOR SPIRITUAL RENEWAL
The pastoral relevance of the Nicodemus Narrative for spiritual renewal is not only important but also timely within current U.S. culture. For several reasons the Nicodemus Narrative remains central for Christian growth.

Encountering God
Encountering God is a process that at times may be quite arduous. The reality that Jesus is trying to communicate to Nicodemus is one that takes place through faith. Encountering God through Christ—the Risen One—is a direct result of *metanoia*, the conversion process, and discipleship. *Metanoia* calls one to transformation, a process that takes time, commitment, and responsibility.

Although the Greek term *metanoia* means "repentance," I will define it the way I do for adolescents: (1) a radical change of mind and heart and (2) a total turning away from sin and the world to embrace God. This is precisely the challenge that Jesus gives Nicodemus, a challenge that bewilders and shocks Nicodemus to his Jewish core. Jesus calls him to new birth, but Nicodemus seems not ready to change his religious paradigm and Jewish horizon. Nicodemus leaves more reflective, perhaps, but apparently unchanged in his way of life. Nevertheless, Jesus does make a profound impact on Nicodemus because he is present at Jesus' burial alongside Joseph of Arimathea (Jn 19:38-39). (Bear in mind that we do not know with exact certitude whether Nicodemus ever accepted Jesus' invitation to be "born again.")

Jesus also calls us to the never-ending work of conversion. Since the People of God are *perfectly imperfect*, it is safe to state that encountering God involves both a struggle and a surrender in order to achieve transformation. Conversion involves three components: intellectual, moral, and religious.2 The entire conversion process is one that culminates in union with God—in other words, completely and absolutely falling in love with God. This is the ultimate goal and prize for the person who responds to Jesus' injunction to be "born again." Hence, conversion is a choice to enter into a personal relationship with God, one that demands a daily response, a desire to change one's life, and a willingness to answer the call to holiness.

The proper response to *metanoia* and conversion is the journey of Christian discipleship. Christian discipleship is the uncomfortable cost of commitment. The Christian call is the call to experience God and to continue Jesus' mission. Christianity is not an experiment to "dabble" in, but is rather a lived reality that one can only acquire from God through Christ and the power of the Holy Spirit.

Living a Life in the Spirit

Since Catholics are "born again" at the celebration of baptism, Catholic religious education and catechetics must implement the Nicodemus Narrative to foster spiritual renewal and Christian growth. The fundamental purpose of spiritual renewal is spiritual awareness and awakening—in other words, living a life in the Holy Spirit. Since the late 1960s, the Catholic Church has experienced a renewal of the Holy Spirit through the Charismatic Renewal, which allows for personal self-discovery of the Holy Spirit as a reality manifested in a Christian's life. This phenomenon of the Holy Spirit allows individual Christians to fully appreciate the enormous impact that the Spirit offers. Pastorally, spiritual renewal involves three criteria: (1) having the Holy Spirit reborn and renewed in one's life, (2) becoming "on fire" for God, and (3) living the effects of the Spirit's indwelling presence. Often these are concepts used in the preparation for confirmation.

Renewing Spirituality

Adolescents need to encounter Christ enthusiastically, and using the Nicodemus Narrative can help religious educators and youth catechists put a new "spin" on regeneration. The creativity and passion of the educator will eventually foster spiritual renewal in the life of the young as well as bring about a spiritual revival within the youth ministry community and the larger parish community. The interaction between Jesus and Nicodemus is most satisfying and offers various pastoral implications. For example, here are three points:

First, Jesus confronts Nicodemus's lack of spirituality and openness to renewal. Jesus challenges his understanding of Judaism and his personal spirituality. In our present Catholic situation, catechists must confront young people about their lapses of spirituality and have a plan to encourage its growth. Once a catechist challenges an adolescent's journey with God, he or she must have a plan to implement and interpret what it means to become "born again" in terms of spiritual renewal.

Second, Jesus invites Nicodemus to share in the Kingdom of God. Jesus insists further that Nicodemus must be "born again" to see, witness, comprehend, and enter the kingdom. Therefore, catechists of youth could emphasize the reality of personally acknowledging what it means to be "born again." Such a declaration professes personal faith, which includes metanoia, conversion experiences, and discipleship.

Third, Jesus' articulation (albeit symbolic) for Nicodemus to be "born again" is a call to spiritual awakening; indeed, each person has to heed the call to spiritual awakening and to be "born again." Adolescents today need tangible tools that spiritually empower them to become more fully attuned to God: tools that help them discover God, change their world view, broaden their spiritual horizons, and shift from typical Catholic catechetical formation to using the Scriptures for personal transformation and increased self-awareness. The "born again" text is such a tool because it causes teenagers to think about their own spirituality, to question their own commitment to God, and to articulate their personal belief about Jesus as the Christ.

Being on Fire for God

"Were not our hearts burning within us while he talked with us on the road and opened the Scriptures to us?" (Lk 24:32). The ending of the Emmaus story depicts the type of fire that excites and ignites Christians who have had a personal religious experience of God. It is no accident that John the Baptist clearly states, "[Jesus] will baptize you with the Holy Spirit and with fire" (Lk 3:16). Both pericopes reference fire to illustrate the profound impact God has on a person who seeks God. Being "on fire" for God is an evangelical phrase that summarizes a personal commitment and encounter with God and is therefore most appropriate to use with teenagers in a youth ministry context.

The symbolism of fire is meaningful to junior and senior high students, especially within the context of a sacred moment. The "fire" inside a teenager is an individual response to the Holy Spirit's presence. It is a fire that comes only from the power, presence, and the person of the Holy Spirit and excites adolescents to put their faith life into action. The inner stirring of the person is the Divine breaking into the heart and soul of the believer.

Showing sensitivity towards the senses and symbols by using fire in youth ministry settings such as retreats and prayer vigils forms a receptive atmosphere for the Spirit's presence to be manifested within a young person's life, provided the space is sacred and has spiritual ambiance. Fire conjures up many images, but when used properly it is a catalyst for prayer and meditation as well as a symbol of God's indwelling presence.3

Experiencing the Indwelling Presence

The effects of the Holy Spirit's indwelling power and presence are uniquely Christian experiences. These effects are enormous because they enable Christians to carry on the mission and ministry of Jesus of Nazareth as well as empower Christians to be of service to the Christian community. The spiritual effects of the Holy Spirit are twofold: (1) the acquisition of spiritual gifts and (2) the achievement of the fruits of the Spirit. Paul encourages followers of Christ to live by the Holy Spirit and not be "ignorant of spiritual matters" (1 Cor 12:1). He encourages the faithful to integrate fully the nine gifts of the Holy Spirit into their spirituality. As listed in 1 Corinthians 12:1-11, these gifts of the Spirit or *charismata* ("charisms" or "ecstatic phenomena") are wisdom, knowledge, discernment of spirits, faith, ability to heal the infirm, miracles (mighty works), ability to speak in tongues (*glossolalia*), interpretation of tongues, and prophecy. These gifts are individual manifestations of the Spirit's indwelling presence but are for the edification and exhortation of the community. They call for both communal and personal character and spirituality.4

The Apostle Paul also mentions the fruits of the Holy Spirit (Gal 5:22-23) as a direct consequence of living in the Spirit as opposed to living in the flesh. According to Paul, there are nine fruits of the Holy Spirit: love, joy, peace, patience, kindness, generosity, faithfulness, gentleness, and self-control. The fruits are characteristics of authentic discipleship. Paul not only encourages spiritual renewal but calls for Christians to be actively engaged in spiritual living. The Spirit directs and moves believers to conform to godly standards and not to worldly values.

IMPLICATIONS FOR YOUTH MINISTRY

As a youth minister, I use the Nicodemus Narrative in various settings to enliven faith, to plant seeds of growth, and to evangelize and catechize adolescents. Whether a five-minute reflection or an entire weekend retreat is designed around the Nicodemus Narrative, the result is spiritual renewal for Christian growth. I found success using this model within adolescent ministry settings for evangelical, catechetical, and spiritual purposes. Each of these categories can involve diverse forms of pastoral praxis. A description of a few successful experiences using this text follows.

Evangelical Purposes

A typical Catholic youth ministry setting in the United States involves a gathering of adolescents, usually at the parish. The gathering is both catechetical and evangelical, and it can include prayers, announcements, ice-breakers, music, skits, a presentation on a particular topic, small-group discussions, and refreshments. It is in this atmosphere that implementation of the Nicodemus Narrative has been most fruitful. The gathering focuses on evangelization. Here is a basic outline for the presentation "Are You 'Born Again'?" or "What Does it Mean to be 'Born Again'?" The catechist

1. Asks a young person to read aloud the Nicodemus Narrative slowly and clearly
2. Leads a two-three minute discussion about the meaning of the text
3. Discusses briefly the theological reality of regeneration (new life in Christ)
4. Shows a three-minute segment of Franco Zeffirelli's 1976 movie *Jesus of Nazareth* (the encounter between Jesus and Nicodemus is found in part III)
5. Discusses Nicodemus's reaction to Jesus' saying, "You must be 'born again,'" especially Nicodemus's look of confusion, despair, and uncertainty
6. Discusses the application and appropriateness of the pericope for today
7. Sends the young people away with something to ponder for the next week or to discuss further in small groups

This is just one example; there are several possibilities. The entire presentation should not last more than twenty to thirty minutes. Although the presentation is geared towards evangelization, the focal point is spiritual revelation—that is, having the participants come to a self-awareness of their own spirituality or lack of spirituality as if Jesus were directly addressing them with the "born again" question.

Catechetical Purposes

One of my favorite catechetical tools for making this pericope "come alive" is Bible study. Many Bible studies are designed for fully initiated adolescents in the

Catholic Church (although some might lack confirmation). The goals of Bible studies are (1) to engage students in pragmatic biblical theology and (2) to empower them for Christian discipleship.

The students who participate in Bible studies are "core students," that is, students who by offering their time and talents are truly invested in youth ministry. Many youth ministries around the United States refer to their core leaders as "peer leaders" or "peer ministers." The point is that Bible studies are usually held separately from the larger youth ministry gathering, and they are part of the ongoing mystagogical faith formation of fully initiated teenagers. Here is a suggested outline for a sixty-minute adolescent Bible study utilizing the Nicodemus Narrative.

1. The youth minister offers a gathering prayer that resonates with the particular pericope being discussed, in this case John 3:1-15.
2. Students brainstorm on the meaning of the phrase "You must be born again."
3. The youth minister asks the students if they have heard that phrase at school or at Church.
4. The youth minister encourages discussion of any negative connotations of the phrase "born again," then casts the phrase in a positive light. Students read the Nicodemus Narrative.
5. The youth minister gives a theological and sacramental explanation of the term "regeneration" by explaining the phrase: "You must be born of water and the Spirit." Youth ministers must carefully present the Church's sacramental perspective (allow 15-20 minutes).
6. The students form three groups:
   Group 1: (a) Read John 3:5-6, (b) list three ways per person that help prove that a person can be born of water and the Spirit, and (c) formulate a nine- to twelve-line theological treatise incorporating verses John 3:5-6 and the proof that a person can be born of water and the Spirit.
   Group 2: (a) Read John 3:8, (b) list three examples per person of the action of the Spirit in their lives, and (c) create a nine- to twelve-line poem incorporating verse John 3:8 and giving examples of living a life in the Spirit.
   Group 3: (a) Read John 3:12, (b) list three practical reasons per person to believe in God, and (c) compose a nine- to twelve-line prayer incorporating verse John 3:12 and giving examples for belief in God.
7. The youth minister then facilitates a large-group discussion around each of the small group's tasks (allow 10-15 minutes). In addition, the facilitation should include a catechetical moment to address any misconceptions or misguided statements that may have come up in the small groups.
8. The minister encourages the students' efforts and gives a final wrap-up.

The Bible study concludes with a sending prayer highlighting what has been learned and shared. The Bible study, although primarily a catechetical instrument, is also a measuring stick for spiritual rejuvenation. The catechetical connection needs to concentrate on the christological and pneumatological aspects of being "born again." There is interdependence between the Risen Christ and the Holy Spirit, which Jesus promises. Thus, spiritual rejuvenation becomes a good starting point for catechesis surrounding the Nicodemus Narrative.

Spiritual Purposes

Weekend retreats are the spiritual backbone of a quality parish-based youth ministry. From my experience, teenagers love to participate in weekend retreats and are even enthusiastic and excited about them. Retreats are another avenue for successfully implementing the Nicodemus Narrative. Utilizing the Nicodemus Narrative can be either evangelical or catechetical for retreat work; however, it should be a primarily spiritual exercise.

For the "born again" pericope to be successful on a retreat, the presentation of the Nicodemus Narrative ideally allows teenagers to experience reverence—a deeply felt reverence for the sacred and a reverence for their own spirituality. Since a retreat is a large block of time, a few different scenarios are recommended. First, the entire theme of the retreat could be marketed as "Being Born Again" or "New Life in Christ" or "On Fire for God." Use whichever theme "grabs" the attention of teenagers and encourages them to participate. Second, the "born again" text may simply be a slice of the entire retreat experience. If this is the case, then either the evangelical presentation or catechetical Bible study may fit rather concretely. Third, the encounter between Jesus and Nicodemus may be the subject of a five-minute morning reflection incorporated within the context of Morning Prayer. The youth's skit ministry or drama club could reenact the story.

A retreat's purpose is to increase the spirituality of a person—that enables them to come to a deeper understanding and appreciation of God and their personal relationship with God based upon their own experiences. Therefore, youth retreats should move adolescents towards the Apostle Paul's mandate: "Be transformed by the renewing of your mind" (Rom 12:2). Such a transformation takes place through various evangelical, catechetical, and spiritual activities, exercises, and mediums.

The Nicodemus Narrative is a magnificent text to use because its spiritual underpinnings are appropriate for Catholic renewal especially within the context of parish youth ministry. The "born again" experience is a spiritual one that fills each of us with awe, inspiration, and illumination. If implemented appropriately it can foster a spiritual revival, stir spiritual awakenings, and be a catalyst for mystical insight among adolescents.

In the final analysis, the "born again" pericope is a tangible vehicle for accepting God in faith. It can lead to the beginning or deepening of a personal relationship with Jesus, the Christ. The narrative also provides a reverent reflection on the masterfully crafted words by Jesus that allow teenagers to reflect on their lives' meaning and resonate with Nicodemus's struggle. Thus the Nicodemus Narrative is a great starting point for adolescent spirituality and catechesis. ❧

1. The entire Nicodemus Narrative incorporates Jn 3:1-15. For the purposes of this article, biblical texts and pericopes, unless otherwise stated, come from the *New International Version: Study Bible* (NIV) (Grand Rapids, Mich.: Zonder-van Bible Publishers, 1995) because it translates the phrase "born again." The NIV normally is not used for catechesis because it does not have an imprimatur.

2. Bernard J. F. Lonergan, *Method in Theology* (New York: The Seabury Press, 1979), 237-244.

3. Ralph Del Colle, "Postmodernism and the Pentecostal-Charismatic Experience," *Journal of Pentecostal Theology* 17 (2000): 107-109. Also see Ralph Del Colle, "The Holy Spirit: Presence, Power, Person," *Theological Studies* 62:2 (June 2001): 332-336.

4. The nine gifts that the Apostle Paul refers to are distinct from the seven traditional "Catholic" gifts of the Spirit that Catholic adolescents are often taught to memorize before the celebration of confirmation. The seven traditional "Catholic" gifts found in Isaiah 11:1-3 are piety, understanding, counsel, wisdom, fortitude, knowledge, and fear of the Lord. One difference between charismata and the seven traditional gifts is that, in the case of *charismata, gratia Dei libere data est* (the grace of God is freely given without restraint), whereas the seven traditional gifts are habitual and related to sanctification and the sanctifying process of the Holy Spirit.

Revisiting Adolescent Catechesis

In the decade and a half since The Challenge of Adolescent Catechesis *was published, much has happened—is happening— that needs to be considered in revising the document.*

By MICHAEL CAROTTA

(Author's Note: Fifteen years ago The Challenge of Adolescent Catechesis *was published by the National Federation for Catholic Youth Ministry in collaboration with the NCEA, the NCDD (now the NCCL), and the then USCC desk for youth ministry. It was a breakthrough document at the time, providing parishes and schools with clarity and direction in the field of adolescent catechesis. It is currently being revised.)*

Aspects of catechesis have changed over the last fifteen years. Then, Catholic parishes and elementary schools were only beginning to recognize that a different approach to catechetics was necessary to reach junior high youths. The catechetical needs of at-risk youth was an emerging topic. Adults with theological backgrounds and religious education training were teaching in parishes and high schools, and the only catechism people vaguely remembered was the one from Baltimore. The themes of peace and justice dominated bishops' pastorals and catechetical curricula, and the RCIA had captured the interest of the best and brightest catechetical thinkers.

A CATHOLIC THEOLOGY OF THE HUMAN

Given the changes in the world over the last fifteen years, it is worthwhile to reaffirm our Catholic theology of the human and its relevance to adolescent catechesis. Both the *Catechism of the Catholic Church* (CCC) and the *General Directory for Catechesis* (GDC) remind us that *all humans have the natural ability to know God*:

Man's faculties make him capable of coming to a knowledge of the existence of a personal God. . . . "Our holy mother, the Church, holds and teaches that God, the first principle and last end of all things, can be known with certainty from the created world by the natural light of human reason." Without this capacity, man would not be able to welcome God's revelation. Man has this capacity because he is created "in the image of God." (CCC, nos. 35, 36)

This theology of the human—that is, this anthropology—is the basis for our understanding of revelation through Scripture and Tradition, our acceptance of faith and reason. In many cases this anthropology distinguishes Catholicism from Protestant denominations.

In reflecting on our positive view of the human in one of my graduate courses, a Methodist student compared this theology with that found in the Doctrinal Standards and General Rules of her faith community:

> Original sin standeth not in the following of Adam (as the Pelagians do vainly talk), but it is a corruption of the nature of every man, that naturally is engendered of the offspring of Adam, whereby man is very far gone from original righteousness, and of his own nature, inclined to evil, and that continually.[1]

A Catholic anthropology believes that adolescents, like all humans, have the innate ability to sense the Sacred and develop a relationship with God. This ability comes with being "created in the image of God" and reaffirms two aspects of our current practice of adolescent catechesis: assume that young people already have a spirituality, and help them further reflect on it in light of the Catholic faith. Catechetical approaches that assume that adolescents are spiritually bankrupt or "inclined to evil" do not reflect a Catholic anthropology.

This is not to say that the Catholic view does not also rightly recognize our innate sinfulness, our innate need for redemption, and the saving influence of grace. It is a view that sees the interconnectedness of human goodness, human sinfulness, and the redemptive power of grace. *The General Directory for Catechesis* states that a world view that does not see God's "goodness [in] all beings; the power of sin which limits and numbs man; and the dynamism [of renewal] which burst forth from the Resurrection . . . cannot be authentically Christian" (no. 16).

A Catholic anthropology underscores our perception of young people and our ministry among them: they too are made in the image of God and flawed by original sin. Because this theology acknowledges that young people already have a faith relationship with God, the tasks of adolescent catechesis identified fifteen years ago are still valid. One task of catechesis is to help young people attend to their existing faith experiences. The other catechetical task is to help them find a home for their faith in our Catholic family. Each task requires different catechetical skills and goals. One focuses on the content of their lives, the other focuses on the content of Catholic identity.

INCULTURATED CHRISTIANITY

The data from most recent surveys tell us that most Americans believe in God, pray regularly, and think they are going to heaven. We are currently riding a national wave of interest in spirituality: angels on TV shows, spiritual readings on bestseller lists, talk-show hosts discussing spiritual exercises, and mediums helping loved ones communicate with the deceased. Spirituality is now part of the public conversation. This was not the case fifteen years ago.

Therefore adolescent catechesis reflecting a "primary" or missionary form of evangelization is no longer as helpful as it once was. What is needed now is a sharply focused catechesis that goes deeper sooner into the spiritual hungers of adolescents. The USCCB's most recent document on youth ministry—*Renewing the Vision: A Framework for Catholic Youth Ministry*—and the GDC share this view: the focus of adolescent catechesis in a culture that already believes should be on discipleship:

> If we are to succeed, we must offer young people a spiritually challenging and world-shaping vision that meets their hunger for the chance to participate in a worthy adventure. . . . We need to provide concrete ways by which the demands, excitement, and adventure of being a disciple of Jesus Christ can be personally experienced by adolescents—where they tax and test their resources and where they stretch their present capacities and skills to the limits. Young people need to have a true opportunity for exploring what discipleship ultimately involves.[2]

The sharp emphasis on discipleship calls us to move beyond catechetical approaches that either spend too much time with self-esteem-building exercises or on preaching to the uninitiated. People already have faith. The focus should be on how to live it, which poses a great challenge to our present images of Church. But this is exactly what John Paul II calls us to, as cited in *Renewing the Vision*:

> This is what is needed: a Church for young people, which will know how to speak to their heart and enkindle, comfort, and inspire enthusiasm in it with the joy of the Gospel and the strength of the Eucharist; a Church which will know how to invite and to welcome the person who seeks a purpose for which to commit his whole existence; a Church which is not afraid to require much, after having given much; which does not fear asking from young people the effort of a noble and authentic adventure, such as . . . following . . . the Gospel. (10)

DEVELOPMENTAL THEORIES

Fifteen years ago the catechetical community was willing to understand faith as a process consisting of certain "phases," "stages," "levels," or "styles" that were sequential. We tried to understand faith as something that developed along an orderly fashion and that coincided with one's increased age and ability to think abstractly. Perhaps it is no longer necessary or helpful to put eggs in this basket. Today it might be more helpful to understand spiritual growth as consisting of three dimensions: (1) the way one relates to God through prayer, worship, and religious practices (vertical); (2) the way one relates to God through moral interactions with others (horizontal); and (3) the way one experiences God's ability to help deal with internal pain, stress, loneliness, fear, sadness, anger, and other emotions (internal).

A three-dimensional view of spirituality might help us understand what seems to be a contradiction among young people (and adults as well). Many young people seem to have a strong vertical dimension of spirituality but a weak horizontal dimension. That helps to explain why, for example, some young people maintain their relationship with God by saying night prayers or attending Mass but are promiscuous. Or why some young people wear rosaries around their necks, yet shoot people who come into their neighborhood.

A weak vertical dimension of spirituality but strong horizontal one help us understand, for example, the young person who doesn't see the need to pray or go to church but strives to be loving, explaining that "what God really wants me to do is be kind to other people."

A weak internal dimension of spirituality might explain how a young person who attends Mass, prays regularly (strong vertical), and lives a moral life (strong horizontal) still needs to "get high" in order to cope with emotions that are either painful or unaddressed.

Some years ago, Michael Warren pointed out that the question is not "Do young people have a spirituality?" but "What kind of spirituality do they have?"[3] Would adolescent catechesis be enhanced if we deliberately attended to a specific dimension of spirituality for a short time, and then turned our attention to another? Would our work among young people be enhanced if we helped them to assess the stronger and weaker dimensions of their spirituality and to develop a personal plan for strengthening their weaker dimension(s)? I believe that young people would find this approach more helpful and empowering. This kind of spiritual development has to be seen as a key part of the journey of discipleship. (This could also apply to adult education.) Given the complexity of today's cultural influences, the faith development theories of the past may not be as helpful as they once were. Understanding spirituality in terms of three different yet overlapping dimensions challenges us to aid adolescents in developing a balanced Catholic spirituality that helps them exercise religious faith, moral living, and emotional management.

CATECHETICAL LANGUAGE

How to find the appropriate language, a challenge facing adolescent catechesis in the new millennium, is clearly described in the *General Directory for Catechesis*:

> One of the difficulties to be addressed and resolved is the question of "language" (*mentality, sensibility, tastes, style, vocabulary*) between young people and the Church (*catechesis, catechists*). A necessary "adaptation of catechesis for young people" is urged, in order to translate into their terms "the message of Jesus with patience and wisdom and without betrayal." (no. 185)

The responsibility for adaptation is on adults, not young people. The difficulty is not just a matter of vocabulary. The "necessary adaptation" must also reflect the "mentality, sensibility, tastes, and style" of young people. How are we to translate the beliefs of our Catholic faith "into their terms" without betraying the richness, mystery, and wisdom of it? I do not know the answer, but I am sure that this is a question worthy of the most thoughtful, imaginative, responsible, and committed minds in the field of adolescent catechesis.

Our current practice of adolescent catechesis emphasizes the role of community to a generation that generally values individual faith more highly. Should the necessary adaptations include turning down the volume of our emphasis on community and turning up the emphasis on discipleship? My experience is that this shift captures the spiritual interest of young people because it is less encumbered and more accessible to them than communal membership. The *General Directory for Catechesis* places emphasis on the Christocentric nature of our faith:

> The fact that Jesus Christ is the fullness of Revelation is the foundation for the "Christocentricity" of catechesis: the mystery of Christ, in the revealed message, is not another element alongside others, it is rather the center from which all other elements are structured and illuminated. . . . The definitive aim of catechesis is to put people not only in touch, but also in communion and intimacy, with Jesus Christ. (nos. 41, 80)

Suppose our catechetical resources and rhetoric emphasized Catholicism as an invitation to discipleship, *then* pointed out our conviction that it is an invitation best lived out in a *community* of disciples? Could some of the "necessary adaptation" include an emphasis on the spiritual resources of our Catholic faith that are very appealing to a generation of spiritual seekers? Would it be worthwhile to emphasize that the Catholic faith is a place of Wisdom? That our faith contains spiritual resources like hope, strength, truth, compassion, love, freedom, irony, imagination, mystery, and moral principles? For a generation interested in *behaviors* (as evidenced by the acceptance of "What would Jesus do?" accessories), could we encourage a return to Christian practices such as honoring the body, praying and fasting, lamenting, focusing on the corporal and spiritual works of mercy, among others?

THE DELIVERY SYSTEM

Over the last fifteen years, the currency of time and the aging process have caused the talent pool of competent, confident, educated, and trained catechists to shrink. In parish-based catechetical programs, adults no longer are willing or able to donate one night a week as a catechist for eighteen to thirty-six weeks. Adults are neither willing nor able to donate the time to attend catechist certification courses. We have invested more time in work and more time in our kids' after-school, evening, and weekend activities.

Adolescents are also dealing with the currency of time. Both females and males are investing more of their time than ever in sports, fine arts, work, and social activities. Fewer are willing or able to commit to weekly catechetical sessions.

Perhaps our parish-based delivery system of weekly or monthly sessions is no longer the richest way to provide adolescent catechesis. Its present design is only effective if volunteers, with their own work and family responsibilities, carve out the time to get trained/certified, prepare ahead of time, and show up once a week to facilitate catechetical sessions for adolescents, who themselves have carved out the time to go to school, do their homework, and pursue their interests and commitments—even if they have already been confirmed and believe (mistakenly) that they have "graduated" from religious education. Not only is the design outdated, but it contributes to the mindset that catechesis is weekly (or monthly) and terminal (ending with confirmation).

Several dioceses are designing a new delivery system that gathers young people from all the parishes in the deanery or region for one catechetical weekend per semester. Young people are asked and expected to block out one Saturday/ Sunday in the fall, spring, and summer. They are given the dates months ahead of time, look forward to gathering with youth from other parishes, and can still attend to the other demands on their time during the week. Some still attend weekly meetings of their choice, like small-group Bible study in someone's home or Sunday night movie discussions.

Only a small number of adults are needed as catechists for these weekend seminars. DREs can draw from a talent pool bigger than just their local parish since it is a deanery-wide event. Those adults who are competent and confident find it much easier to commit for a weekend than for one night every week. They can get the materials far in advance and have plenty of time to prepare. Some can be trained for just one specific catechetical weekend and study only the doctrinal content related to the topic(s) of that one weekend course.

DREs find quality control easier to manage in this format. Instead of relying on the particular personality of each catechist, DREs can supply the catechetical team with lesson plans that employ both inductive and deductive methods, allowing the team to serve as mediators between the participants' life experiences and the contents of our faith, and taking into account the influence of group dynamics, media, and active participation as suggested by the *General Directory for Catechesis* (nos. 116-118, 148-161). New, short-term, intensive models of adolescent catechesis respond to both the shrinking talent pool of catechists and the currency of time. While there is some trade-off with such formats, they represent a delivery system that no longer asks the parish to depend on that which the culture no longer supplies.

The GDC also calls us to reflect the spirit of initiation in catechesis. This presents an intriguing opportunity for Catholic high schools that build a religion curriculum according to academic grade level. For high schools who are willing to explore a new model that reflects the spirit of initiation, consider this: What would happen if the curriculum was built along the lines of evangelization, catechesis, and service (or pre-catechumenate, catechumenate, and *mystagogia*), and students took courses that were more in line with their prior religious education background and current degree of faith readiness than their grade level? Sophomores, juniors, and seniors might be in the same class. Not all juniors will take the course in prayer. New questions would have to be addressed: How do we determine a student's current level of faith readiness? How do we determine when someone is ready to move to a different level?

We developed this kind of program during my four years as religious education coordinator at Boystown High in Omaha, Nebraska. It brings a new set of scheduling dilemmas but makes for consistently engaging religion classes and teacher-student conferences. I know this model can work. I'm sure we can find others if we seek them.

Fifteen years ago we began to get *clarity* around the essential elements of adolescent catechesis; it is now time to develop *intentionality* in our work. How and when are we intentionally helping young people gain religious knowledge? How and when are we intentionally developing Christian attitudes? How and when are we intentionally promoting Christian behaviors? We must attend to the vertical dimension of spirituality (prayer/worship/religious affiliation) as well as the moral dimension of spirituality. We must intentionally make the necessary adaptations to our language in order to translate it into the terms used by adolescents. And finally, we must intentionally focus on discipleship to meet the catechesis needs of adolescents today. ❧

1. Harriet Jane Olson, et al., eds. *The Book of Discipline of the United Methodist Church 2000* (Nashville: The United Methodist Publishing House, 2000), article VII, 87.
2. National Conference of Catholic Bishops, *Renewing the Vision: A Framework for Catholic Youth Ministry* (Washington, D.C.: United States Catholic Conference, 1997), 9, 10. Subsequent references are given in the text.
3. Michael Warren, *Faith, Culture, and the Worshiping Community* (New York: Paulist, 1989).

A Catechumenal Model for Confirmation

In the case of adolescents, a confirmation program modeled on the OCIA is an invitation to inquiry, illumination, and appreciation of the sacrament.

By TOM WASHBURN

The challenge of catechesis is to evangelize and catechize adolescents effectively. On the surface, today's adolescents often appear disinterested in the Church and religion, and we assume it will be difficult to teach them. But is it possible that working with adolescents, preparing them for confirmation, involving them for the rest of their lives in the Church may be easier than we assume? The answer is yes. When today's parents were children, the Second Vatican Council recognized the need for church documents to be attentive to the signs of the culture around them and sought a way to communicate the life-saving Gospel of Jesus Christ in a way that each culture and age could understand. In this article, I suggest a catechetical program that has had success achieving these goals at my parish in New Hampshire. Before describing that program, however, I will present the context of adolescent catechesis and define the spiritual hunger felt by teens of this generation.

CATECHESIS AND CONFIRMATION

The Order of Christian Initiation of Adults (OCIA) (in the United States, the initials RCIA are still commonly used) is excellent in its realization that people do not come to faith through a learning that is akin to the academy, but rather through a personal experience or encounter with people who are excited about faith and want to invite others into an experience of that exciting faith. Adolescents likewise need to see that faith is something relevant and helpful. By modeling adolescent catechesis on the OCIA model of invitation, inquiry, illumination, and sacrament, confirmation can become a new beginning for this young generation. At 1995's World Youth Day, Pope John Paul II defined this new beginning for the Church:

> What is needed today is a Church which knows how to respond to the expectations of young people. Jesus wants to enter into a dialogue with them and, through his body which is the Church, to propose the possibility of a choice which will require a commitment of their lives. As Jesus with the disciples of Emmaus, so the Church must become today the traveling companion of young people.[1]

The U.S. Catholic bishops followed the pope's comments with their own statement, *Renewing the Vision: A Framework for Catholic Youth Ministry*, which outlined three challenges: (1) to empower youth to live as disciples of Christ in today's world, (2) to draw young people to responsible participation in the life, mission, and work of the faith community, and (3) to foster the personal and spiritual growth of young people.[2]

Too often on the parish level young people go through the sacramental conveyor belt. Once the sacrament of confirmation has been administered, they are absent from the Church until another sacramental "moment"—usually marriage or the baptism of a child. In this absence a great opportunity is missed. The current generation is hungry for meaning, hungry to be agents of positive change. Nothing meets this hunger better than faith in Jesus and full and active membership in the Church. In *Novo Millennio Inuente* (apostolic letter issued at the close of the Great Jubilee of the Year 2000), John Paul II challenged youth to preserve our faith:

> Young people . . . have a profound longing for those genuine values which find their fullness in Christ. . . . If Christ is presented to young people as he really is, they experience him as an answer that is convincing and they can accept his message, even when it is demanding and bears the mark of the Cross. For this reason, in response to their enthusiasm, I did not hesitate to ask them to make a radical choice of faith and life and present them with a stupendous task: to become "morning watchmen" (cf. Is 21:11-12) at the dawn of the new millennium.[3]

We catechists need to employ new approaches to reach adolescents and effectively invite them into full membership in the church community. We are challenged to find ways to communicate the Gospel to a community that has never heard it in their language. We cannot assume that we have with youth a base of shared religious knowledge received from parents, family, and Church. We must share the message of Christ as though it has not been heard with a community that listens differently than in the past. Renewing the Vision recognizes the changing needs and approaches to catechizing and evangelizing youth.

m programs to people.
ıristian *bar mitzvah*—a
ation. Adolescents are
d in full membership.
l must stress a greater
ng the young and their
e theology of the sacra-
ı truly communal event
confirmation interview,
ople into the active life

ı born after 1980) are
t describes postmodern
n, connected): "Experi-
ıst half century much of
(driven by things) to a
ınomy (which traffics in
e *on the Church in the*
ponsibility of reading the
the Gospel" (no. 4). Yet
ne-dimensional learning

t life is, especially expe-
om structure does not
adolescents into a com-
be experienced—"faith"
ook.

the textbook, the Church
images on the walls of
atues in city squares, the
Today the technology has
we must enter a story to
ı model of initiation with
hing; in fact his disciples
theological exploration is
t the beginning point for
ractive catechesis was and
ıe Parable of the Prodigal
Millennials can connect.

The 1986 catechetical resource *The Challenge of Adolescent Catechesis* highlighted the need for a stylistic change in adolescent initiation: "The primary aim of adolescent catechesis is to sponsor youth toward maturity in Catholic faith as a living reality. . . . Adolescent catechesis is the process of journeying with young people toward increasing maturity as Catholic Christians."[5] We must apply to adolescent catechesis the same lessons learned from the Order of Christian Initiation of Adults. OCIA creates a sense of membership in the Church personally, catechetically, spiritually, and liturgically. Faith sharing, interactive and engaging catechesis, a life connection—these methods all work well with adolescents.

The challenge for catechesis is to bridge the gap from *what is* to *what is hoped for*. The desire to have programs that can be clearly judged by objective standards—such as requirements fulfilled, papers written, books read—is much safer ground than a desire for programs that seek to discover if someone has set foot on the journey of life with Christ. The criterion for that assessment is subjective but, I think, ultimately a more worthwhile criterion to pursue for the faith lives of adolescents.

SPIRITUALITY OF THE MILLENNIAL GENERATION

- Consider themselves believers, not necessarily belongers
- Focus on discipleship, not membership
- Emphasize the spiritual journey, not organized religion
  - Are open to transcendence, mystery, beauty, compassion, inclusivity, and justice
  - See spirituality as withdrawal from the rat race, competition, hatred, judgmentalism, and violence
  - See religion as judgmental, elite, abstract, and boring
- Feel that the experience of Church and its Jesus is critical
  - See Jesus as one who understands their suffering, not as a best friend
  - Want persons who speak of Jesus to be supportive and caring
  - Want to focus on individual relationships with Jesus
- Desire to experience the transcendence and power of God
  - Need spiritual experiences (World Youth Day, National Catholic Youth Conference) and a spiritual context (parish)
  - Believe that Hollywood knows! (MTV, *The X-Files*, *City of Angels*, *Field of Dreams*, *The Matrix*)
  - Use the arts and nature to discover God in videos, dance, music, sculpture, stories, art
- Want to share their spiritual journey with others who are supportive, welcoming, authentic, and caring

—Robert McCarty, Executive Director
National Federation for Catholic Youth Ministry

My parish of St. Thomas Aquinas in Derry, New Hampshire, has more than 10,000 members on its roster. The religious education program serves 1,200 young people annually with 200 catechists. In addition to catechetical programs, St. Thomas has an active youth ministry program that works with young adults and junior high and high school youth to meet their spiritual, service, and social needs. Our former program involved a traditional two-year, academic-oriented confirmation program that culminated in the all-important confirmation staff interview to discuss the following: the sacramental nature of confirmation, the involvement of *confirmandi* in the community, the knowledge learned, etc. It was a highly ineffective process, not quite what *Lumen Gentium* (*Dogmatic Constitution on the Church*) was looking for: "By the sacrament of Confirmation [the baptized] are more perfectly bound to the church and are endowed with the special strength of the holy Spirit" (no. 11). Many programs seek to make youth into theologians rather than initiate them into the community.

We shifted our understanding of this task from being part of a *program* run by *teachers* for *students* in the academic model to being a formation model that speaks of religious formation (not education), faith-seekers (not students), and catechists (not teachers). Never underestimate the power of our words. We looked at active adolescents for the common denominator of their experience. We have many adolescents active in the liturgical assembly as lectors, Eucharistic ministers, music ministers, servers, masters of ceremony, leaders of our children's Liturgy of the Word, members of our parish liturgy committee, and so forth. They are ministers serving their peers alongside qualified adults. They are religious "formators" to younger children. They train new altar servers, work in outreach programs, and more.

Active adolescents shared a few characteristics. They experienced themselves as members of the community—almost always through personal connection. Someone of faith made a difference in their lives that connected them to the community. Most had attended our Teens Encounter Christ (TEC) retreat. Most had been invited by parish leadership to use their gifts in the community.

We evaluated our program in light of *Renewing the Vision*'s assertion that *"all ministry with adolescents must be directed toward presenting young people with the Good News of Jesus Christ and inviting and challenging them to become disciples"* (10). We identified areas of concern like the lack of integrity of the sacrament of confirmation—we had been acting as if it were more important to confirm young people ("conveyor belt" logic) than to challenge youth to discipleship. When this great event of full membership in the Church is populated by strangers, it loses its symbolic and sacramental value.

RECOVERING CONFIRMATION

We agreed that not everyone *must* be confirmed at the end of the program. Instead, only those who *desire* confirmation receive it. Easier said than done. Anyone who has encountered parents whose only concern is that their child be married in the Church while not being particularly interested in whether the child participates in the faith can understand the dilemma. This program required a great deal of education of the parents as well. We also need to re-orient our catechists. Somehow confirmation had become a rite of graduation *from* the Church, not commencement *into* fuller membership in the Church. Confirmation was a fond farewell to those whom we barely knew.

We focused on trying to recover a sense of confirmation as intrinsically tied to the process of initiation. Most parishes have experienced the success of the Order of Christian Initiation of Adults and yet failed to apply those lessons to other initiation programs. "As our vision of religious education becomes more holistic," writes Francoise Darcy-Berube, "our approach to it becomes more pastoral. We realize increasingly that our efforts on behalf of religious education should be less fragmented, more global, more coordinated and comprehensive; they should bring about more cooperation, more sharing of ideas, responsibilities and resources."[6] The model of our programs should develop informed disciples whose lives are formed by the Gospel, whose parents have a role in the formation process, and who are integrated into the life of the community.

The quote from Luke's gospel quickly comes to mind as the goal of our new vision: "Were not our hearts burning [within us] while he spoke to us on the way and opened the scriptures to us?" (Lk 24:32). This is the experience of discipleship for which we strive, rather than striving instead merely to show in our files that young people had turned in the requisite paperwork and attended the correct number of classes. We want young disciples!

In our new program, aptly called Burning Hearts, confirmation is emphasized as part of the sacraments of initiation. It is a good chance to make young people feel like members of a community of believers, to light a spark of faith in their lives, to invite them into the mystery of God's love for them, and to help them embark on a life-long journey of faith growth and exploration. If there is an overarching theme to this program, it is community. Young people will enthusiastically enter full membership in the Church if they see that they are welcome and that this faith can change their lives. Once that goal is accomplished, they will want to know more about our faith, so post-confirmation catechesis (*mystagogia*) is another important element in this program. Like the Order of Christian Initiation, we seek first to invite and then to allow for a period of inquiry, a period of catechizing, a period of purification and illumination, a completion of initiation (confirmation), and a life of continued involvement in the community.

BURNING HEARTS

While still holding true to the requirements set forth by our diocese, Burning Hearts seeks to adapt and present the process of preparation for confirmation in a way that youth can apprehend and make their own. The program centers around three areas: worship, service, catechesis. All three of these *foci* orient the youth towards community. The first adaptation is that all events happen within the context of the parish. In the past, religious education students would hold separate prayer services, complete individual service projects, and spend a lot of time in isolated learning. These are not bad things in and of themselves, but they don't serve the goal of membership in the community.

In terms of worship, youth are expected to attend Mass weekly as well as work to foster their own prayer life and spirituality. Youth also sponsor worship events for the parish during the year that range from evenings of Eucharistic devotion to Lenten stations of the cross, as well as other ideas they bring to the community. Youth also attend a yearly retreat.

Many of the same youth service projects still exist; but instead of doing something separate from the community, youth invite others to join them in a service activity as well as participate in service activities offered by the parish. Young people's serving side by side with older members of the community is a beautiful thing to watch, as one mature generation realizes and supports the faith of the new generation. By working side by side, youth come to know the type of service in which their faith community engages.

Catechetically, the content is the same, but the context is radically different. Catechesis takes place in a more interactive and engaging environment. The new approach builds in greater flexibility. The curriculum is divided topically and offered in four-week blocks at different times and on different days to work within the busy lives of youth. This flexibility has also increased the number of adults involved, as many people can commit to a four-week mini-course but not a two-year program.

Another area of change in the new program surrounded the traditional confirmation interview. The Diocese of Manchester asks that each young person being confirmed meet with a member of the parish staff prior to confirmation. But instead of an individual interview, we developed communal sessions. Over the course of four evenings, we invited groups of twenty youth along with catechists, members of the parish staff, and one or two confirmed youth into the rectory for prayer, conversation, and dinner. These sessions began with prayer led by the young people and were followed by introductions, a basic sharing by the parish staff about our hopes for and understanding of this moment, and then a chance for genuine conversation. Halfway through we broke for pizza and refreshments. These communal sessions effectively modeled a greater sense of community and connectedness. The atmosphere was more engaging and less intimidating. Adolescents were encouraged to share, discuss, and ask questions as they approached this faith moment.

We developed a helpful explanation: "Confirmation: Gifts of the Holy Spirit: A Tool Box for Believers." A summary of this program follows:

> Our lives of faith are difficult. Our world challenges us all the time. How will we be up to the challenge and strengthen our faith? God gives us some gifts—Wisdom, Understanding, Knowledge, Fortitude, Counsel, Piety, Fear (Awe) of God. We always have a choice to use [these] gifts or not. If we don't use them, they can't strengthen us. Just because we're given gifts, doesn't mean we know how to use them. We are part of a community of believers so that together we can learn to use them and strengthen our faith lives. When we think of the challenges in our lives, the gifts of the Spirit are really those things that help us meet the challenge. Wisdom— [gives you] the ability to know what God wants you to do. Understanding—helps you know what God has revealed to human beings. Knowledge—gives you the ability to understand and accept things as they are. Fortitude—provides you with

special strength and courage to deal with life's trials. Counsel—helps you to decide what to choose and what to do in touchy situations. Piety—helps you to honor God as a good and loving Creator. Fear of God—gives you power to love and show reverence to God in all you do. These gifts must be learned and lived in community.

We stress the prayerful and service-oriented nature of the Church, as well as the need for these confirmed youth to see this sacramental event as a starting point. One primary question was asked of youth: Where will you fit into this community after confirmation? We revamped our retreat structure to address our new approach. Building on our EPIC model, the Lukan story of the disciples on the road to Emmaus who encounter the Risen Lord and see him in the opening of Scripture and the breaking of the bread seemed like the most obvious choice. Emmaus is an EPIC moment. The disciples experience Jesus in multiple and interactive ways and came to see who he was and who they were in relation to him—they were connected.

The content of our youth retreat did not differ much from a TEC retreat. The conceptual focus remained on the Paschal Mystery, sacraments, prayer, Christian living, and reflections on confirmation and the gifts of the Holy Spirit. But the context of the retreat was drastically altered. Our approach was to get to know these young people on a personal level, to make connections with them, and to invite them into a community of believers. We focused on continual community-building activities, stressed personal interaction and discussion, and celebrated prayer and worship services that were engaging and structured in a way that spoke to youth sensibilities. We placed a greater focus on what they needed to know and express than on our need to dispense dogma.

We also involved as much of the parish as we could. One strategy involved keeping the parishioners aware of the process the youth would follow during the year through bulletin articles, Mass announcements, prayer petitions, mentions in homilies, and so forth. Additionally, we invited the whole parish to write letters to candidates, offering prayer and support. Many parishioners also dropped off baked goods and the like for retreatants during the weekend, and we pushed for large parish attendance at the confirmation ceremony.

On the retreat, we highlighted confirmed teens who offered personal witness on how all of this information and connection had affected their lives in concrete ways. Retreatants had opportunities for personal reflections in journals, in small- and large-group discussion, in prayer petition, on posters, and in other ways. Time and again it was the personal witness of peers that made the deep connection with the retreatant teens, and it was these connections that continue to resonate with these young people now months after their confirmation.

CREATING DISCIPLES

I am not implying in this article that these changes to our confirmation program have suddenly created perfect disciples, but the difference between this year and prior years has been evident. The comments I received show that young people have made a connection with a community and with a faith experience that was perhaps a first-time event for them. After seven years of continuous religious education, they finally felt like members of this group of believers. These young people have also had a great desire to be involved in a continued way and at a deeper level in the life of the church community.

As *Renewing the Vision* concludes,

> The Church and world need the faith, gifts, energy, and fresh ideas of young people. The entire Church, and in a special way ministry with adolescents, must empower young people for their mission in the world. . . . All of our efforts to promote an active Christian discipleship and growth in Catholic identity must lead toward mission. We pray with the whole Church that we can meet the challenge of *Gaudium et Spes*; ". . . the future of humanity lies in the hands of those who are strong enough to provide coming generations with reasons for living and hoping." (50-51)

The key to effective adolescent catechesis in the Church in the United States is to trust in the work that God can and will do in the lives of youth if we participate with him in the task at hand. It is sometimes frightening to enter new ground with our youth programs; but once we make that leap of faith, it may be that in addition to bringing youth into activity in our Church, we will ourselves be led by their growing faith.

As the pope wrote, "I did not hesitate to ask them to make a radical choice of faith and life and present them with a stupendous task: to become 'morning watchmen' (cf. Is 21:11-12) at the dawn of the new millennium" (*Novo Millennio Inuente*, no. 9). We catechists must participate with Pope John Paul II in preparing these "morning watchmen" for the tasks that lies ahead. The challenge of creating young disciples is not a difficult one, but it must be a personal one, taken up by the whole community in an effort to draw young people into a life of faith. ✒

1. John Paul II, *Youth: Sent to Proclaim True Liberation*, Address at World Youth Day 1995 (Philippines).

2. National Conference of Catholic Bishops, *Renewing the Vision: A Framework for Catholic Youth Ministry* (Washington, D.C.: United States Catholic Conference, 1997). Subsequent references are given in the text.

3. John Paul II, *Novo Millennio Inuente* (2001), no. 9. Subsequent references are given in the text.

4. Leonard Sweet, *Post-Modern Pilgrims: First Century Passion for the 21st Century Church* (New York: Broadman & Holman Publishers, 2000), 33. Subsequent references are given in the text.

5. National Federation for Catholic Youth Ministry (NFCYM), *The Challenge of Adolescent Catechesis: Maturing in Faith* (Washington, D.C.: NFCYM, 1986), 1. *The Challenge of Adolescent Catechesis* was developed in collaboration with the National Catholic Educational Association, the National Conference of Diocesan Directors of Religious Education (now the National Conference for Catechetical Leadership), and the desk for youth and young adult ministry of the Department of Education, United States Catholic Conference.

6. Francoise Darcy-Berube, *Religious Education at a Crossroads: Moving on in the Freedom of the Spirit* (New York: Paulist, 1996), 19.

The Coach as Catechist:

YOUTH AND SPORTS

The diocese of Belleville, Illinois, has completed a pilot program that introduced catechetical or religious education elements into the sports programs serving children of the diocese.

By MARK S. MARKULY

An estimated twenty-five million American children participate in athletics every year. But according to a survey of 26,000 youths by the Institute for the Study of Youth Sports at Michigan State University, 75 percent drop out of what had been their favorite sport by the time they reach fifteen years old. The children said they threw in the towel because it wasn't fun anymore and blamed the reason for quitting on coaches who yelled, played favorites, and emphasized winning at all cost. In September, a nine-year-old boy in Crown Point, Indiana, returned the trophy he won for the 1995 state championship team to the Little League board. "The coaches treated me like scum," he said. "I don't want this."[1]

Another aspect of the emotional pressure on youth in sports programs is the attitude and behavior of parents, which is often worse than the coaches who are obsessed with winning. Unfortunately, inappropriate behavior in sports events is not restricted to secular Little League programs. Many youth in Catholic sports programs have similar experiences to tell.

Given the parish and school resources devoted to sports, how exactly does athletics fit into the mission of the Church? Does it fit in at all? Or, does it violate the mission? Should the Church foster a "theology of competition"? When do coaches, players, and parents cross the line into non-Christian actions and even cause psychological and spiritual damage to youngsters? Do church-sponsored sports witness for or against the Gospel?

Religious-sponsored sports leagues exist in the shadow of secular sports, a multibillion dollar industry that uses the best techniques in advertising and public relations to manipulate the attitudes and desires of potential consumers. Of all the activities sponsored by churches, sports buys into powerful cultural forces, making an uneasy alliance between the principles of Christianity and dimensions of the entertainment pastime.

CHRISTIAN SPORTS: AN OXYMORON

What would Jesus say about the phenomenon of American sports and its murky relationship with sports programs for youth? Would he agree with a man who criticized a Catholic coach because she stressed ethical behavior with her players? "You Christians don't belong in sports because the world is not nice," he told her recently. "You're teaching these kids that if they go out for something they're going to get to play even if they're no good. Well, what good does that do them down the road?" Is a Christian sports team in twentieth-century America an oxymoron?

Throughout history, Christianity has excelled at putting a "God-spin" on the secular interests of its people, placing a new layer of meaning on an activity and connecting it with the teachings of Jesus. St. Paul, for example, took up the images of the stadium and athletic competition to express the meaning of apostolic ministry and fidelity to Christian life and its goal: running, shadowboxing, training (1 Cor 9:24-27); seeking the prize (Phil 3:14); competing for the crown (2 Tm 4:7-8). These images appealed to the Greek audience familiar with gymnasia and games. But is it possible to put a "God-spin" on sports as they are played in today's world? Or is this one cultural force too strong for even the dynamics of the Gospel? Before answering, consider the depth of the challenge. Sports have a power to rival Caesar's.

Sports programs shape the financial priorities in school systems at the elementary, high school, and university levels and reach into both public and private sectors. The monetary and legal gymnastics required by the rather conservative city of St. Louis to purchase the Los Angeles Rams a few years ago demonstrates how sports can get entire cities to mortgage their future. The seductive power of this industry, however, lies in its influence on less tangible, more precious commodities than political and social institutions. Sports mold the dreams and values of our children in ways we cannot measure. In 1991 teens listed two sports figures among the top three "most admired men": first Magic Johnson and third Michael Jordan (then-President George Bush was second).[2] A more apparent measure of the influence of sports celebrities is witnessed each year in our children's insatiable appetites for the outrageously priced consumer goods hawked by professional athletes.

JESUS OVERTURNS THE GOALPOSTS

When Jesus overturned the tables of the money-changers in the temple, he reminded of priorities.

The Diocese of Belleville, Illinois, invoked Jesus to overturn the goalposts of its sports programs. A chief goal was to get parents, coaches, and parishes to look at priorities. In April 1996, the diocese completed a pilot program that introduced catechetical or religious education elements into the sports programs serving children of the diocese. The program, entitled *Win the Prize,* asked athletic leaders to serve as more than just teachers of sportsmanship and the skills of soccer or basketball. Coaches were asked to envision themselves as catechists and religious leaders and their team as a small faith community. *Win the Prize* was used in all the diocese's sports programs serving fifth through eighth grades.

The inspiration for putting catechesis and athletics together came from listening to ministers in the field. Parish directors of religious education find themselves competing with sports for time and funding. Through a sports-catechetical program the diocese set out to refashion athletics as a support system for the more formal catechetical efforts.

The key to *Win the Prize* is this: Elements of Christian teaching and references to God are invoked in the heat and commotion of the real-life situation of a competitive practice and game. Coaches, players, and even parents are given an opportunity to "do Christianity" on their feet, rather than just talk about it in the cerebral, reflective mode of desk or pew. Theological reflection and *lectio divina* tango with the soccer ball.

EVANGELIZING COACHES

When the idea of a program merging elements of religious formation and sports was first discussed with athletic directors and coaches three years ago, it was not greeted enthusiastically Some leaders feared a hidden agenda of foisting the responsibility of failed religious instruction on athletics. Others believed the sports culture was irreconcilable with the Gospel. But all agreed that most Catholic youth—and their parents—had far more energy, excitement, and commitment for sports than for ongoing religious education and formation. If a parish offers an evening of adult education it is lucky to draw ten to fifteen people. But a gathering to discuss an issue about sports can fill the church.

Win the Prize was designed to evangelize and catechize the coaches and their players by making use of four traditional components of catechesis: word, worship, community, and service. In the summer and fall 1996, some eight hundred coaches in the diocese were taken through a mandatory three-hour training session explaining the program. The training was required for coaching certification. Many did not come willingly. In the first year, coaches were asked to integrate at least one of the four components into their coaching.

The biggest challenge in the program design was finding ways to have coaches feel comfortable using catechetical elements in practices and games. Most existing religious education materials are too intimidating to take coaches on their first step toward becoming a catechist. The two-year development of the *Win the Prize* materials operated on the principle of keeping the materials as simple and basic as possible.

AN AWKWARD ROLE

But even with the simplicity of the *Win the Prize* program, most coaches found their new role awkward. At the end of the pilot year, a survey and interviews of the urban and rural coaches revealed their thoughts and the way they implemented the project. Eleven percent of the coaches said they felt extremely uncomfortable and 34 percent admitted to being at least a little uncomfortable serving as the faith leader of the team. Another 52 percent of the coaches said they were uncomfortable talking about Jesus.

"I saw *Win the Prize* as a good way to help others," a coach in the Belleville diocese said in a postseason focus group. "[But] it's a very uncomfortable thing to stand up as a coach and to say: 'How about faith?'"

"This was really neat, but I was really scared, too, because I thought, 'Oh, my God, [what] if I have to quote . . . Scripture,'" added another coach.

To ease the coaches' transition in identity, *Win the Prize* included a pledge that parents had to sign at the beginning of each season. The pledge informed parents that the parish sports program was an extension of other religious education efforts in the parish and would serve as part of their youngster's religious formation. Parents and children were expected to abide by Christian principles and participate in the catechetical dimension of the team. The purpose of the pledge was to put the weight of the parish and the diocese behind the coaches' new role and to serve as a notice that the days of running sports programs with no spiritual accountability were over. Coaches reported in the survey that more than 56 percent of the parents were receptive to the pledge, with only 5 percent unreceptive.

THE GAME OF LIFE

Another resource for the coaches' new role as catechetical leader was a small booklet called *Xs and Os: The Game Plan of Life*. The booklet provided small Scripture passages and reflections for the coach to use with the team before and after the practices and games. Reflections were written intentionally to add no more than two or three minutes to play time. It was assumed from the beginning that getting Catholic coaches to read and reflect on Scripture in front of their team would be difficult. Athletic leaders who have served as coaches for five years or longer are most likely to describe themselves as "competitive" and seem more likely to resist the idea of using the Bible in their coaching duties than are new coaches.

"I'll be honest with you, I'll probably never grab a book and read a Scripture out of it," a coach of many years said. "And I don't think any of the coaches would do that. I really don't, because everyone who is coaching now grew up in the system where you teach the kids the fundamentals, you teach the kids how to win or lose gracefully. If they learn that then they'll know no one is going to give them anything in life and they're not always going to win."

But, contrary to the coach's skepticism, over 20 percent of the coaches did use the Scripture passages at "every" or "most" practices, and another 10 percent used them at less than half their sessions, according to the coach survey. Another coach making use of the Scripture meditations before and after practices was surprised to find his players very interested in the new spiritual component to the team's activities: "We did [the Scripture pieces] religiously" he said. "Everyone wanted to be the one who did the reading. That's really hard to believe. We had fifth-, sixth-, seventh-, and eighth-graders all wanting to be participating in that. I found that pretty amazing."

Even more amazing to this coach were the teachable moments developing from the Scripture passage and reflection. Some youth asked questions like, "What does that mean?" But more frequently players would ask, "Why are we doing it this way, while the school who played us last night and thumped us real bad is playing the way they are?" The query provided an opportunity to discuss the difference between a team's playing by Christian principles and one's playing by the rules and goals of the secular sports culture. "I think for some of them it was one of the first realizations where the outside world is," the coach said.

Given the emotional intensity of athletics, coaches are in a unique position with their players to suggest the Christian tradition as a guide for living. How often do players approach their coaches with requests for counseling or guidance? More than the designers of the program expected. Coaches reported discussing critical issues with their students: divorce, family concerns, God and going to church, drugs and substance abuse, and illness and the death of a loved one. More than 19 percent of the coaches reported that they had occasion to discuss all the above issues with their players at one time or another.

To aid the coaches in finding inspiration and role models for their shift from mere teacher of a game to religious leader, the *Win the Prize* program included small stories in a section called *Chalktalk*. The stories gave anecdotes of Christian professional athletes who have used their wealth and fame as a platform to share their faith in Jesus Christ. Nearly 46 percent of the coaches found the stories helpful to envision their new role.

TURNING THE TEAM INTO A FAITH COMMUNITY

In addition to the various attempts to introduce Scripture and prayer into the rhythm of practices and games, each team was asked to attend a Sunday Eucharist or other worship and to do a service project as a team. These two elements were designed to help shape the sports team as a community of faith, as well as a team of players.

The pilot year suggested coaches in the *Win the Prize* program were most open to expressing their faith through worship. Only 3 percent of the coaches did not go to worship, while 42 percent reported it was a positive experience.

The service project did not fare as well. Although 43 percent of the coaches surveyed reported doing the project, 48 percent did not. But some went beyond the program's expectations. One coach from an urban area took his entire team for an overnight trip to help clean up a summer camp operated by the diocese. Four parents went along for the experience. The team returned the following evening and attended Mass together at their home parish. Another coach, who went along on the excursion but had reservations about the entire *Win the Prize* program, found the young people's willingness to work inspiring. "I was kind of skeptical about it [doing the service project], and I said, okay let's try it. But then after I saw it, and saw some kids that I would never have dreamed of helping out and chipping in, and worrying about their buddies . . . it was kind of surprising to me."

BREAKING DOWN THE STEREOTYPE OF CATHOLIC COACHES

Everyone engaged in the catechetical ministry realizes from experience how difficult it is to do religious education in our consumer culture. The *General Catechetical Directory* recognized that new approaches are needed for new times (no. 9). If Catholics are to pass faith on to the next generation, parents must see the religion teacher as one dimension of family and parish spiritual formation. But, despite many years of discussion about the entire parish participating in the religious education process, few parishes are able to engage most parishioners with this vision.

An exciting aspect of developing the *Win the Prize* program was the opportunity to compile a profile of Catholic coaches and to explore the possibilities of enlisting this group of men and women into the Church's catechetical mission. Though sports are one of the most popular activities in the Church, attracting far more parishioners than most other programs offered by the parish, little is known about the people who run Catholic athletics. Even less is known about the potential "teachable moments" of practice sessions, games, and tournaments.

When discussed in ministry circles at all, sports programs are usually treated as a troll under a bridge: "If at all possible, avoid it altogether and take the long way around." Coaches are often stereotyped as drooling Neanderthals, scraping their knuckles in the dirt as they pace the sidelines and hurl profanities at young children. Though excesses exist and many parishes have at least one coach who has a win-at-all-costs attitude, research in the Belleville diocese has revealed that many of the common ideas about Catholic coaches are in fact caricatures.

The *Win the Prize* experiment has demonstrated that most of the men and women who volunteer in the Church as athletic coaches are a wonderful, caring, and fun-loving group of people. The majority carry the Golden Rule in their heart and desire to act with honesty, fairness, integrity, and compassion. Most try to "do the right thing," as one coach put it, by trying to teach children "the values that they need and what they're going to need to be better people in life." Even fiercely competitive coaches can become tearful remembering moments when they helped a child feel more confident or secure. Such coaches just feel their job is to work with the best athletes, much as teachers work with the best students for other extracurricular competitions like spelling bees or math contests.

CHRISTIAN SPORTS: AN IGNORED RESOURCE

Win the Prize worked far better the first year than expected, based on the results of a survey, focus group, and individual interviews with coaches in the diocese. The research before and after implementing the program supports the initial belief that our children need to see faith lived, discussed, wrestled with, and expressed in the context of doing the things they want to do and while watching adults do the things adults want to do.

In implementing *Win the Prize* diocesan leaders learned the best coaches in the diocese were already using some elements of the program. These women and men felt affirmed by the diocese's attempts to put faith at the center of parish sports activities. But, it appears even the best coaches are not involved in adult religious education programs offered by their parishes or the diocese. Catholic coaches live their faith based on their ideals. Until now, few athletic leaders have seen the need to better understand those ideals by exploring the Catholic tradition in a formal way.

In developing *Win the Prize*, the designers wanted to see if the materials would entice coaches to seek out a deeper understanding of their faith and the faith of their Church. It is too early to see how well it accomplished this objective, but it is clear the program got many adults in the diocese to start talking about issues of their faith. School boards and parish councils had many discussions about the program, some heated. The program also changed the behaviors of some of the crustier athletic leaders.

A competitive coach, who expressed fear that the sports-catechetical program would spoil the excitement and fan support at games, nevertheless credits *Win the Prize* with convincing him to return to Mass. "When we started [*Win the Prize* in the diocese] I wasn't very good about going to church on Sundays a lot of time," he said. "But since we started this program I feel like I've got a responsibility to go to church on Sundays. I think the kids around here are begging to look up to somebody. I think there's a few people that they do [look up to]. And I hope I'm one of them. I think when they see me in church it helps to give them a good impression."

Despite the successes of *Win the Prize* in its pilot year, it has a long way to go to reach its full potential. The average coach will have to learn the "faith skills" to make the most of the catechetical opportunities in his or her coaching. To use a sports metaphor: If Christianity is to offer an alternative to the powerful cultural force of the sports industry, it will need coaches who can perform on the varsity level of faith leadership and faith expression.

---

1. *Family Circle*, April 23, 1996, 94.
2. *America's Youth in the 1990s* (Princeton, N.J.: George H. Gallup International Institute, 1993), 161.

Being Faithful—
Pursuing Success

TOOLS OF ASSESSMENT

Social science tools and testing instruments like the NCEA's
ACRE are helpful at measuring "success" and suggesting how
catechetical efforts may be more effective.

By M A R K   S .   M A R K U L Y

Many catechists take courage from a saying attributed to Mother Teresa (during periods of trial and frustration): "We're called to be faithful, not successful." Focus on what you do, the Albanian nun suggested, not on your perception of the results of your labor. These are wise words for any minister.

In the mid-1990s, D. C. Wyckoff and G. Brown Jr. discovered that the most prominent religious education theories of this century were intellectual composites of many academic and practical disciplines: philosophy, the arts, creativity, psychology, technology, adult religious education, to name only a few.[1] A number of models have risen to the surface from the confusion, but all make claims on the effectiveness of their methods with little empirical evidence.[2] As a result, in the past four decades the field of religious education has developed a type of attention deficit disorder, with a kind of chaos of competing theories for what works and does not work in catechesis. The confusion of the field was penetrated in 1999 when Tom Walters wrote an article for *The Living Light* called "Catholic Literacy: A Modest Proposal."[3] Walters clarified the distinction between educational outcomes in religious education (learning knowledge about the tradition and developing Catholic literacy) and catechetical outcomes (learning born of initiation experiences). This article explores the practical side of the "Modest Proposal": how do we really know what religious education outcomes we can accomplish, and more importantly, what instructional practices most effectively help us accomplish those outcomes? The answers will not come easily, but applying social science tools and perspectives to the ministry of catechesis provides some insights. The first step to such an application is making better use of religious education testing instruments like NCEA's Assessment for Catholic Religious Education (ACRE) or the Catechetical Assessment Program's Faith 2000, the official standardized test for the Archdiocese of Indianapolis.

Gathering empirical evidence through testing instruments and other evaluation tools gives the researchers the ability to separate fact from opinion and therefore to eliminate generalizations, biases, misplaced assumptions, and faulty perceptions or logic. For more than a decade the traditional academic disciplines—reading, writing, math, science, and social studies—have sharpened the professionalism of their fields with educational evaluation and research. Social science's tools have helped the standard K-12 subject disciplines to articulate more specifically and realistically the goals and objectives of their efforts, and to identify the "best practices" for achieving those goals and objectives. Teachers from many disciplines of study have learned how to have more outcome-oriented discussions. They have become more sensitive to the practices that promote real learning among students. They have honed skills in motivating students to use knowledge at higher levels of thinking, and they have created habits for experimenting with methodology and content in a systematic fashion that promotes their own growth as educators.

With all deference to Mother Teresa, looking to "success" as well as faithfulness is important, and since 1993 the Diocese of Belleville in Illinois has tried to gather empirical evidence of the "success" of its religious education efforts in both schools and parishes. If the word "success" is too grating, with its connotations of power and mercantile advancement, replace it with "effectiveness." As James Michael Lee so thoroughly demonstrated in his trilogy on religious education in the 1970s and '80s, on the level of such things as creating learning experiences, promoting understanding of concepts, structuring curriculum, and evaluating effectiveness, studying a faith tradition has many similarities to studying other subjects.[4] Whether in a liturgical catechesis setting, a pilgrimage or service experience, an RCIA gathering, or a traditional classroom discussion of the faith tradition, catechesis has a necessary dimension of traditional learning, and the process of learning follows certain patterns and principles that are structured into human consciousness.

In the process we have had successes and have also learned to identify some of the potholes in the terrain. The biggest pothole is that the interface of religious education, faith, and social science is a tough sell to the catechetical community. Most catechists and catechetical leaders have a hard time imagining Jesus or the apostles pouring over statistical tables, interview and focus group transcripts, religious education assessment scores, or portfolios to better understand how to preach the Gospel more effectively to the Pharisees, Saduccees, Zealots, Essences, or Gentiles. Connecting matters of faith with social science can also resurrect specters of the nineteenth-century faith-and-reason debates, or create suspicion that the purveyors of the scientific method are once again trying to encroach on the sacred territory of faith. Worse yet, it can send up a flare that the diocesan bean counters are once again attempting to wield a business model of accountability into matters of the soul that are beyond their model's comprehension.

Religious educators can improve instruction by utilizing empirical data, especially from religious education standardized tests. But optimum use of these data requires an appreciation for several distinctions that have evolved over three decades in the evaluation field and more than ten years of educational inquiry into best practices in the major K-12 academic disciplines. The first distinction is the difference between a teacher or service focus and a student-learning or client focus. The second is sensitivity to the three distinct choices of evaluation methods in using a testing instrument: summative, formative, and knowledge-oriented. The third is a heightened awareness of the difference between evaluation logic and the logic employed in the theological disciplines. Awareness of these three distinctions opens up new vistas on the importance and usefulness of empirical tools, especially religious education assessments.

SHIFTING THE FOCUS FROM TEACHER-ACTION TO STUDENT-LEARNING

With reading and writing leading the pack, educators have advanced their understanding of the most effective ways to promote learning by shifting the focus of attention from what the *teacher is doing* to what the *student is learning*. In the evaluation field, this is sometimes referred to as a distinction between a service-centered (or teacher-action) focus and a client-centered (or student-learning) focus.[5]

Mother Teresa's contrast between faithfulness and success can highlight this distinction. An evaluation of faithfulness is teacher-action- or service-focused. It is interested in the type of textbooks used, the number of contact hours with students, the annual turnover of catechists, the number of parents attending catechetical functions, and the budget devoted to religious education. It is interested in the kinds, amounts, and quality of service offered. Outside of feedback sheets on workshops and religious activities, most church evaluations and formal research are service-centered.

Although this is valuable information for understanding trends in the field, teacher-action- or service-centered evaluations do not yield the kind of data needed to improve the effectiveness of religious education instructional practices. Such improvement will only come through student-learning- or client-centered measurement and evaluation, which ask the truly tough questions of instructional practice and outcomes:

> What results are my religious education efforts actually accomplishing with my students? After completing a good and energetic learning experience, how do I determine whether my students were educated and not merely entertained? What elements of the faith tradition engaged youth and adults, and which did not? Why? Which of my learning experiences created an emotional bonding with the tradition, and which did not? How did my learning experiences actually impact the practical realities of my students' lives, helping them create templates of meaning that will bring a sense of grounding and direction to the chaos of this period of history. Lastly, what are the real factors that help my students—young or old—engage the Spirit of the living God within the context of the rituals, beliefs, stories, art forms, music, and ancient personalities of the faith tradition?

These student-learning- or client-centered questions seek to understand how our "service" impacts our "clients": What do the student and disciple do with the learning experiences we lay before them? How does this learning impact their thoughts, feelings, and actions? What are the further questions those experiences awaken in their hearts and minds, and what is the most effective way to engage that budding curiosity?

These kinds of questions rub against the grain of many religious education efforts. Little wonder Mother Teresa's words resonate with many a struggling catechist. Worrying about faithfulness "feels right" for the catechetical enterprise because it hearkens to one of the more popular images of the ministry: the Parable of the Sower (Lk 8:4-15). Sow your seeds faithfully. Let God handle what happens with the seeds of faith you sow.

Assessments and evaluations led by student-learning questions are terrifying to any devoted educator. For many reasons—some good and defensible, and others bad and inexcusable—few catechetical leaders pursue these kinds of questions. But it is precisely because we do not pursue student-learning- or client-centered empirical data that I believe many catechists and catechetical leaders in parishes, schools, and diocesan offices feel like the ancient mythical figure Sisyphus.

Sisyphus, a King of Corinth, was condemned to Hades to forever roll a boulder up a hill, only to have it roll back down each time he reached the top of the hill. The monotony and frustration of Sisyphus is reflected in the "circles of frustration and concern" that stalk catechetical discussions. For the most part, the same circles in 1980 still haunt catechetical conversations. Our litany may be similar:

> Youth become disinterested in religion during adolescence; too many parents demonstrate little to no interest in parish activities, including attendance at the

Sunday Eucharist; most people seem to struggle with connecting church doctrine and the practical challenges of daily living; and a religious illiteracy plagues all age groups. In addition, there is the high turnover in parish catechists each year, the insufficient number of professionally trained religious educators, the chronic concern about improper funding for religious education needs, the feeling of second-class status for parish-based programs compared to the Catholic school, etc.

These circles of frustration and concern have changed little in twenty years. The same boulders are rolling up and down the hill, because little new practical information on effective instructional practice has been collected that might lead to solutions to these problems, or at least a greater clarification of the questions most likely to lead to the answers. Only a student-learning, client-centered focus will ultimately lead to the insights needed to break through these circles of frustration. The Diocese of Belleville moved in this direction by making use of survey or testing data.

MOVING TO A STUDENT-LEARNING FOCUS BY TESTING STUDENT LEARNING

The Diocese of Belleville has learned that one of the best ways to begin a tradition of "measuring" the effectiveness of catechetical efforts is to make use of an instrument like ACRE or Faith 2000. Both instruments offer user-friendly tools for collecting religious education data.

In 1993 the Diocese of Belleville began using ACRE to move toward a student-learning focus, discovering immediately that the data gathered by such instruments provide no immediate indication of what needs to happen to improve catechesis. But we have found that the data can help us begin a new type of discussion about catechesis and provide some benchmarks of what's actually happening in a community's efforts to pass the tradition on to youth. The knowledge sections of the data provide a good barometer of the effectiveness in passing on vocabulary and basic concepts, and the more affective questions offer a sounding board for such things as attitudes, perceptions, and practices that directly or indirectly reflect the practical life of faith.

Although the ACRE materials suggest the use of the data to check performance outcomes, I have found that most schools and nearly all parishes are not interested in this approach. Instead, I have found the data particularly valuable in creating thoughtful discussion on the nature, purpose, and effectiveness of religious education with virtually any group of people in the Church. The discussion of Walters's possible outcomes—real and imagined—can occur within the context of some real data on what is happening with youth.

The process of using testing data began for the diocese with a developmental comparison of ACRE data from fifth-, eighth-, and eleventh-grade students in the

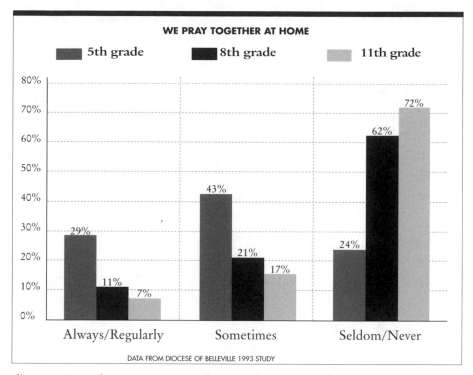

diocese. Annual reports compared more than seventy items from the ACRE instrument. Most of the items had a graph and an accompanying small discussion on the possible relevance of the findings to religious education instructional practice. Because the testing occurred with different groups of youth, there was no pretense of proving any developmental trends. Rather, in the absence of such trends, the data were presented to create discussion. Consider the following graph of student responses to the item: "We pray together at home."

Such a graph allows for a more convenient way to pose a penetrating question to catechists and catechetical leaders: Assuming the ACRE results are trustworthy and accurate, what challenge does this data pose to our religious education instructional practices? According to students, communal prayer in Catholic households ceases or drastically decreases between fifth and eighth grade. If this is true, how can parishes and schools promote the importance of communal prayer and provide engaging or meaningful options of family prayer? This question creates new opportunities for changes in instructional practice, as well as justification for a new emphasis in the overall curriculum.

What is the potential for making use of something as simple as a graph to promote a change in thinking and practice about religious education to catechetical leaders, catechists, parish councils, school boards, or parent gatherings? Parker Palmer suggests the possibilities. In one college course, Palmer spent two weeks with a simple four-cell statistical table that related income to race as the launch pad for in-depth classroom discussions. Assuming it was a three-hour course, one table offered six hours of content, using a methodology that required the student to do the thinking:

> With this table at the center of our circle of inquiry, I taught by asking question after question about it. As the process unfolded, I tried to wait out the silences until responses came; to engage students in dialogue with each other, not just with me; and when the discussion became terminally tangled, to sort things out with a "lec-turette," always followed by a fresh round of questioning and conversation.[6]

The diocese has learned that using empirical data to guide instructional decision making is guaranteed to meet initial resistance in certain places. One resistance I have noticed among religious educators is to immediately question the wording of a testing item or question, rather than what the item responses might suggest for changes in their own instructional practices. In the case of the diocesan statistics on family prayer, many school catechists protested that they had often sent materials home to parents but received no feedback. The teachers assumed the parents were not interested in faith practices in the home, an assumption that was supported by the teachers' observations of low attendance by many parents at the Sunday Eucharist. In response, the diocese created its own parent survey to crosscheck the parental perspective on the same subject. Interestingly, while the teachers believed parents were not interested in getting suggestions for home practices, the survey indicated the majority of parents wanted such suggestions and did not believe they were receiving them!

Empirical evidence highlighted a radical difference in perception on the part of teachers and parents. In response, a diocesan template for parent meetings was developed to improve communication between teachers and parents. In addition, a series of catechetical home aides, taking the form of a type of "sacra-mental," was created to help parents conduct meaningful discussions with their children about faith and the more important issues in life.

CHOOSING BETWEEN THE THREE EVALUATION
CHOICES FOR EMPIRICAL EVIDENCE

Effective use of a religious education survey, or any assessment tool, requires a sense of the three different ways empirical evidence can guide decision making. When most people are told an evaluation is planned, they think in terms of the first type: *summative evaluation*. This type of evaluation is judgment-oriented, seeking to determine merit and value. For many program directors or educators, this kind of evaluation is the fearful harbinger of a termination squad. Summative evaluation often uses data gathered from assessments to decide whether an employee is worth retaining or a program is worthy of continued funding.[7]

In reflective moments, clergy and catechetical leaders usually ask summative evaluation questions about religious education. Is my current director of religious education getting the job done? Is the religious education program working? Does a Catholic school do a better job at religious education than a parish-based delivery system? Most of the scant research that has been done on the effectiveness of religious education is guided by these judgment-oriented summative questions, specifically whether religious education actually helps retain Catholic youth as they move into adulthood. Unfortunately, the results are conflicting and inconclusive.

In the 1960s and '70s, Andrew Greeley found a high correlation between a person's Catholic school attendance and his or her return to the Church after leaving in his or her late twenties.[8] As a result, Greeley decided Catholic schools were amazingly effective in passing on the faith tradition. But Greeley's interpretation of his data had an interesting dark side. He found that religious instruction itself seemed to have little direct effect on the religiosity of returning Catholic young adults. Instead, the primary factor accounting for adult religious behavior was a general sense of "feeling at home" in a Catholic environment. It appeared young people who left the Church came back primarily because as children they were around things Catholic so much that it created a familiar feeling of being at home with the Catholic community.

Greeley had less favorable things to say about parish-based religion programs, maintaining there is no correlation between youth's attending PSR or CCD classes and their return to the Church as an adult. In fact there is often a negative correlation. Assuming a person leaves the Church in his or her late twenties, statistics show that the more PSR or CCD classes that person has attended, the less likely they are to return to the Catholic faith community (Greeley, 253-254). As of 1979, Greeley concluded, parish-based programs, as "a substitute" for Catholic schools, were "simply a waste of time" (254).

On the other hand, a more recent summative evaluation study led by James Davidson indicated that Catholic schooling had a consistent "Catholicizing" effect on youth only when the young person attended twelve or more years of Catholic schooling. Overall, the empirical effects of Catholic schooling were "small and inconsistent," supporting more than three decades of other studies in conflict with the Greeley findings.[9] In Davidson's research, Catholic schooling had its greatest impact in affecting an adult's devotional practices, such as participating in the more Scripture-oriented Bible studies and prayer groups, which were emphasized in the post-Vatican II Church instead of older practices like novenas and the rosary.[10] However, attendance at parish-based CCD or Catholic schools seemed to have an almost equal impact with this type of adult practice. Similarly, a somewhat controversial 1994 study comparing Catholic schools and parish-based programs found only a *slight* advantage in religious knowledge responses between Catholic school students and youth attending parish-based instruction.[11]

I am convinced that the dynamics of effective religious education are still too undefined, and the few professional assessment instruments too primitive, to do summative evaluation. Andrew Thompson's observations about parish religious education in 1986 might very well be true of all religious education: too few researchers have studied the specific situations to make reliable empirical statements about virtually any aspect of religious education programs.[12]

Using assessment tools for *formative evaluation* provides better opportunities for religious education because formative evaluation is improvement oriented. This kind of evaluation is focused on responding to needs, modifying organizational structures, and improving quality. It seeks to improve the structure by searching for both strengths and weaknesses. In most cases, formative evaluation gathers information for a specific period of time, usually at the beginning of a program or in the pilot stage of a project, with the intent of improving implementation, addressing unforeseen problems, or tracking the programs' or participants' progress toward stated outcomes.

Most diocesan efforts evaluating parish and school religious education programming are closest to a "type" of formative evaluation. They search for data on a catechetical program's compliance with the Church's official vision of catechesis as described in catechetical documents, or provide a process for getting systematic feedback on the strengths and weaknesses of various elements of a catechetical program.[13] Shortly after the 1997 edition of the *General Directory for Catechesis* (GDC) was released, Berard Marthaler wrote an article outlining the GDC criteria for evaluating religious education that can serve as a template for principles guiding these types of evaluations.[14] Using ACRE results as they were in the table above is also an example of a formative approach to making use of empirical data.

Since 1994, the Diocese of Belleville has used the ACRE instrument as one of several tools in doing a *knowledge-oriented* or *cumulative evaluation* of religious education. Knowledge-oriented evaluation has the primary goal of "influencing thinking about issues in a general way." The merits of this type of evaluation are that it can influence the parameters of a debate, the language used in discussing the objectives of a field of endeavor, and "the ideas that are considered relevant" to a discussion of improving understanding and practice.[15]

Knowledge-oriented evaluation focuses on the creation of theory. It looks at data with the intent of formulating a theory to explain reality and guide practical efforts to improve instructional practices. Because of the paucity of existing theories to guide the practicalities of religious education, the most frequently quoted theories are products of more academic research and have few direct practical applications. For instance, James Fowler's work on stages of faith tries to posit a schema for how faith development looks and acts. Fowler does not address at all the teaching methods or curriculum structures that might promote a systematic growth in faith stages.[16] Tom Groome has probably had the most profound impact on a distinctive religious education instructional methodology. Although his theories are theologically sound, I know of no empirical evidence that demonstrates its effectiveness in promoting student learning at various age groups and in specific learning situations.

Yet because religious education does not employ an "evaluation logic" for discerning effectiveness and ineffectiveness, many instructional methodologies are referenced as if they do have this empirical evidence. For instance, a rough draft of Groome's Youth Ministry Religious Education Goals referenced shared praxis as defining the methodology for catechesis with youth. I deeply respect Groome's thought and have used it, but I believe its true value for guiding instructional practice will only occur when religious education starts looking at this method through the prism of student-learning-centered evaluation.

When the Diocese of Belleville started using ACRE in a comparative study eight years ago, the primary focus on the evaluation was to look for positive or negative developmental patterns that might identify beginning stages of the disenchantment of Catholic youth with the Church. The hope was to catch young people's first signs of alienation from the faith tradition and to begin designing developmentally appropriate responses. The Office of Education in the Diocese of Belleville issued extensive annual reports on ACRE in 1993-94, 1994-95, and 1995-96, highlighting patterns of intellectual and behavioral shifts in youth beginning in middle school. A theory emerged:

At the outset of puberty, it appeared, many youth were beginning to feel no longer connected to the Catholic Church and its tradition of faith. These initial feelings of alienation culminated in the gradual erosion of retained cognitive, informational, or conceptual knowledge about the tradition between eighth and eleventh grade.[17] In other words, the diocese theorized, the Church began to lose youth at the *affective level* as they moved into junior high school and continued to lose them at the *cognitive* or *subject content level* between eighth and eleventh grade.

Diocesan findings were cross-referenced with a review of the middle school and/or junior high school literature and were summarized in a conclusion that guided efforts to improve instructional practice: *Young Catholics' declining interest in their faith tradition during the middle school years is primarily a problem with the presentation of the social and emotional or "affective" content of the Catholic tradition.*

This theoretical conclusion culminated in several attempts to improve catechetical effectiveness in presenting "affective" dimensions of the faith tradition. One effort constituted bringing some of the content of religious education to one of the more "affect-rich" environments of gathered middle school youth—sports.

This effort led to the development of the nation's first Catholic sports-catechetical program, *Win the Prize*, which was published by Concordia Publishing. The first-year evaluation of this program was reported in a previous edition of *The Living Light*.[18] Another effort arising from the diocesan theory was the creation of a three-hour video series entitled *Enduring Faith*.[19] The video-assisted learning program explored how the Catholic community in the diocese responded and grew in the midst of the rampant racism of the twentieth century.

THE REAL CHALLENGE: CHANGING THE WAY WE THINK

It only takes a short walk down the path of evaluation based on empirical evidence to improve religious education practice to realize that the real challenge of using assessment tools is helping catechists and catechetical leaders become comfortable with empirical data. This requires a different way of thinking, a type of *evaluation logic*. Such logic rubs against the grain of the equally important type of logic that underpins the theological sciences. Unless the distinctions between these different types of logic are exposed, understood, and recognized for their unique gifts to the catechetical mission, empirical assessment is unlikely to help improve instructional practice in catechesis as it has in other learning disciplines.

In the 1970s, James Michael Lee wrote about the fundamental distinctions between the thinking processes and approach of the theological enterprise and those of a social science perspective, which he believed was more suited to addressing the practical needs of religious education. The former makes deductions from principles or assumptions, while the latter must reason inductively from empirical facts. Lee illustrated the distinction with a quote from Josef Jungmann on the most popular catechism in Germany during the late nineteenth century. Joseph Deharbe, who wrote that catechism, operated from a pedagogical principle that abstract truths had to be taught as such and not watered down. Jungmann defended this position in the following way:

> As a result of the careful ordering of these associated parts [in the catechism] the good news character of the dogmatic structure will be made apparent. Through unswerving concentration on what is taught the chances are that the children will remember the basic facts of the Christian faith, even under the most unfavorable circumstances.[20]

Jungmann's statement makes pedagogical assertions from the perspective of a speculative, theological methodology. Consider how he frames his argument:

1. By ordering the catechism in a certain way, the good news contained in dogmatic statements will become apparent to the learner.

2. Through a rigid faithfulness to the catechetical text's instructional design, the elements of the tradition presented in any given class or course will find their way into the long-term memory of the youth.
3. The structure of the curriculum is so thorough and pedagogically sound that it will work in virtually any social or cultural situation.

These are huge assumptions about how teachers teach, how curriculums work, and more importantly, how humans learn and remember.

As a theologian thinking like a theologian, Jungmann did not need to prove his assertions with empirical data. He only needed to make it "reasonable," which he did. As it turns out, forty years of social science research has demonstrated rather conclusively that most of his assumptions about learning, curriculum, and teaching were inadequate.

Jungmann wrote in the late 1950s, prior to Vatican II, but contemporary religious educators still validate their references to religious education methods with reasonable assumptions that lack empirical data. In her recent work, *The Prophetic Spirit of Catechesis*, Anne Marie Mongoven, OP, asserts "that symbolic catechesis is an *effective approach* for many individuals and communities" at this point in U.S. history.[21] Symbolic catechesis connects the symbols of human events and experiences with the symbols of faith, like the Bible, the teachings, worship, and lived life of the Church. Mongoven's reasons for the effectiveness of symbolic catechesis are speculative, not empirical. She cites three reasons for the reader to agree with her assumption. There are no references of studies done on particular texts or catechetical materials that have used the symbolic catechesis approach and demonstrated effectiveness. The author lists her reasons as to why the theory of symbolic catechesis addresses certain cultural and historical needs, and she builds the rest of her remarks on those assumptions. Her points, while theologically sound, for the most part lack empirical substantiation.

Most instructional decisions in parish and school catechesis are guided by the experiences or hunches of catechists or catechetical leaders. In the best situations, a strong theological logic is also employed. But, in the worst-case scenario, instructional and programming decisions are made based on anecdote, founded on personal opinion, or developed through the persuasion of the most charismatic or impassioned personality at the table. In such a situation, enthusiasm and conviction can replace careful planning, systematic exploration of what is really occurring in any given learning moment, and a solid logic to guide decision making.

In one of the most recent national inquiries into the catechetical ministry (CARA's *A Profile of Catechetical Ministry Today*), what worked in religious education was explored solely through the *opinions* of pastors and directors of religious education.[22] As important as these data are to the field, the practical problem solving of pedagogy and programming also requires empirical evidence into what is actually learned by students. Such evidence is scarce, and a great deal of exploration with formative and knowledge-oriented evaluations will have to occur to refine and discover tools for improving our understanding of how best to help students do that learning. In the meantime, existing instruments like ACRE and Faith 2000 offer us a good starting point. The new revision of ACRE, which has made use of the best in empirical testing and evaluation logic, opens new possibilities for both formative and knowledge-oriented insights into the best instructional practices in religious education. An existing summary of some national patterns with the previous generation of ACRE suggests some new questions that need to be asked about what works best and why.

Three decades ago James Michael Lee pointed out that the field of religious education has made little professional exploration of effective and ineffective pedagogy and that it has developed few principles each catechist must follow and questions he or she must ask to determine whether instruction is *actually* creating a learning moment. This is still true in 2001. Recognized instructional principles do not exist for guiding the planning, modification, and evaluation of religious education instructional practice, or overall program effectiveness, or "success," in religious education.

A student-learning focus in evaluation is committed to deepening the understanding of what students *have actually learned, integrated, and applied to their thought processes, feelings, attitudes, and behaviors*. With such understanding, catechesis can still use the metaphor of the Sower in its ministry. But, we can also learn together the most effective ways to nurture the shoot, observe it for growth, and give it the optimal chances for growth.

Empirical assessment is the most powerful path to tackle these new duties of religious education in the twenty-first century. Testing is an important dimension of this empirical data gathering and analysis. It can begin to help catechesis develop a clearer sense of focus, overcome our attention deficit disorder from too many influences, and set religious education on a path to making slow, steady improvement in instructional planning and practice. Tools for making systematic improvement in instructional design and practice exist and have brought benefits to many types of learning. But these tools have not begun to reach their potential for improving the "success" or effectiveness of catechetical efforts. ⚬

1. Cf. D. C. Wyckoff and G. Brown Jr., *Religious Education, 1960-1993: An Annotated Bibliography* (Westport, Conn.: Greenwood Press, 1995).

2. Cf. G. T. McKenna, *Models and Trends in Religious Education* (Mystic, Conn.: Twenty-Third Publications, 1998).

3. T. P. Walters, "Catholic Literacy: A Modest Proposal," *The Living Light* 36:2 (Winter 1999): 59-71.

4. J. M. Lee, *The Shape of Religious Education* (Birmingham, Ala.: Religious Education Press, 1971); *The Flow of Religious Education* (Birmingham, Ala.: Religious Education Press, 1973); *The Content of Religious Education* (Birmingham, Ala.: Religious Education Press, 1985).

5. Mary Patton, *Utilization-Focused Evaluation: The New Century Text* (Thousand Oaks, Calif.: Sage Publications, 1997), 154-162. Subsequent references are given in the text.

6. P. Palmer, *The Courage to Teach: Exploring the Inner Landscape of a Teacher's Life* (San Francisco, Calif.: Jossey-Bass, 1998), 129.

7. Patton, *Utilization-Focused Evaluation*, 65-68.

8. A. Greeley, "My Research on Catholic Schools," *Chicago Studies* 28:3 (1989): 254. Subsequent references are given in the text.

9. W. V. D'Antonio, "Identity and Various Subcultures in the Church Today," in *Evangelization, Culture, and Catholic Identity*, W. Friend, J. D. Davidson, A. A. Zukowski, and M. J. Himes, eds. (Saint Leo, Fla.: Saint Leo College Press, 1996), 95-96; T. Walch, *Parish School: American Catholic Parochial Education from Colonial Times to the Present* (New York: Crossroad, 1996), 232; P. H. McNamara, *Conscience First, Tradition Second: A Study of Young American Catholics* (Albany, N.Y.: SUNY Press, 1992), 135; J. H. Fichter, *One Man Research: Reminiscences of a Catholic Sociologist* (New York: John Wiley, 1973), 221-222; G. Lenski, *The Religious Factor* (Garden City, N.Y.: Doubleday, 1963), 270-271.

10. J. D. Davidson, A. S. Williams, R. A. Lamanna, J. Stenftenagel, K. M. Weigert, W. J. Whalen, and P. Wittberg, *The Search for Common Ground: What Unites and Divides Catholic Americans* (Huntington, Ind.: Our Sunday Visitor, 1997), 102.

11. G. Elford and R. Murphy, *Toward Shaping the Agenda: A Study of Catholic Religious Education/ Catechesis* (Washington, D.C.: Educational Testing Service, 1994), 62-75.

12. A. Thompson, "Research on the CCD," in *Renewing the Sunday School and the CCD*, D. C. Wyckoff, ed. (Birmingham, Ala.: Religious Education Press, 1986), 66-67.

13. A good example of this is the Archdiocese of Chicago's evaluation process *Harvesting Hope*. Most of the assessment criteria are taken from church documents. See the "Self-Study Program" for the Archdiocese of St. Louis.

14. Berard Marthaler, "Measuring Success in Catechetical Programs" *America* 181 (October 2, 1999).

15. C. H. Weiss, "Evaluation for Decisions: Is Anybody There? Does Anybody Care?" in *Debates on Evaluation*, M. Alkin, ed. (Newbury Park, Calif.: SAGE Publications, 1990), 176.

16. C. Dykstra, "Faith Development and Religious Education," in *Faith Development and Fowler*, C. Dykstra and S. Parks, eds. (Birmingham, Ala.: Religious Education Press, 1986), 269.

17. M. Markuly, *Keeping Our Youth Connected to the Catholic Faith: A Summary and Interpretation of the Past Five Years of ACRE Results in the Diocese of Belleville in Illinois* (Belleville, Ill.: Diocese of Belleville, 1999).

18. M. Markuly, "The Coach as Catechist: Youth and Sports," *The Living Light* 34:2 (Winter 1997): 65-71.

19. Salt River Production Group, *Enduring Faith: A Story of African-American Catholics in the United States* (Dubuque, Iowa: Harcourt Publishing, 2000).

20. J. A. Jungmann, *Handing on the Faith*, A. N. Fuerst, trans. and ed. (New York: Herder and Herder, 1959), 143.

21. A. M. Mongoven, *The Prophetic Spirit of Catechesis: How We Share the Fire in Our Hearts* (New York: Paulist Press, 1959), 117-145.

22. M. E. Bendyna, B. T. Froehle, and J. L. Wiggins, *A Profile of Catechetical Ministry Today: Diocesan and Parish Perspectives* (July 2000): 45-53